THE THREE STRATEGIES OF THE

UNSTOPPABLE

WOMAN

For Kathy
May your inner
unstoppable woman
shine brightly

AVIVA
PUBLISHING
NEW YORK

BRITT SANTOWSKI

The Three Strategies of the Unstoppable Woman

© 2010 by Britt Santowski

Published by: Aviva PublishingLake Placid, NY; 518-523-1320;
www.avivapubs.com

Address all inquiries to: 6511 Stonewood Dr, Sooke BC, V9Z 0Y6 CANADA,

Library of Congress Cataloging-in-Publication Data

    Santowski, Britt.
    The Three Strategies of the Unstoppable Woman / Britt Santowski
    290 p. cm.
    ISBN 978-1-935586-11-1
    Library of Congress Control Number (LCCN): 2010923930
    1. Business 2. Entrepreneurship 3. Women I. Santowski, Britt. II Title.
    BF

All rights reserved. No part of this book may be reproduced or transmitted in any form or by any means, electronic or mechanical, including photocopying, recording or by any information storage and retrieval system, without written permission from the author, except for the inclusion of brief quotations in a review. Scanning, uploading or otherwise distributing this book via the Internet or any other means without permission of the author is illegal. Please purchase only authorized electronic editions and do not participate or encourage electronic piracy of copyrighted material.

The author of this book's intent is to help you in your quest to pursue the future of your desires, either as an professionally or in pursuit of your dreams, which may be entrepreneurial in nature or otherwise. In the event you use any of the information in this book for yourself, which is your constitutional and inherent right, the author and publisher assume no responsibility for your actions or outcomes.

The author may be contacted at author@TheThreeStrategies.com

Ordering Information: To order additional copies, contact your local bookstore or visit www.TheThreeStrategies.com.

Quantity discounts are available

First Edition, 2010

50 40 30 20 10 9 8 7 6 5 4 3 2 1

Editor: Lori Stephens

Final Edit and Proofreading: Tyler Tichelaar

Publishing Coach: Patrick Snow

Interior and Cover Design: Fusion Creative Works

WHAT OTHERS ARE SAYING ABOUT

THE THREE STRATEGIES
OF THE UNSTOPPABLE WOMAN

"*Unstoppability* is what separates those who try from those who do. This book gives women the key to joining the league of those who do."

— **Mary West**,
Contributing Author of *Your Ultimate Sales Force*

"Unstoppable people are ones who can bring their dreams to reality. This book shows the way."

— **Alan Roaf**,
Current Coaching Consultant and
Former National Coach of Canada's Olympic Rowing Teams

"Britt Santowski is a leading authority on the subject of strong and successful women. This book conveys her undeniable passion and knowledge. Britt connects with her readers unlike anyone I have ever known. Let her show you how to become unstoppable using the three strategies that are sure to change your life forever!"

— **Malika L. Anderson**,
Author of *The Real Woman's Guide to an Almost-Perfect Life*

"Climb or catapult towards your success. This book lays a solid foundation for your exponential growth."

— Patrick Snow,
International Best-Selling Author of *Creating Your Own Destiny.*

"*The Three Strategies of the Unstoppable Woman* is that book women have long awaited—a surefire guide to finding the required balance in life that leads both to goal-achievement and happiness."

— Tyler R. Tichelaar, Ph.D.,
Author of the Award-Winning *Narrow Lives.*

"Packed with what I call Green Light® actions, Santowski's superb tools help you get the GO-ahead. Use them to live your dreams - on or off the motorcycle."

Marilyn Schoeman, Author of
GO! How to Think Speak and ACT to Make Good Things Happen

"Kudos to Britt Santowski. She offers a fresh perspective on strategies for living your best life and a framework of practical **Calls to Action** that will inspire you to dig deep and connect with the unstoppable woman you can be."

Jane L. Thilo, M.D., M.S.

DEDICATION

For

Vincent Cummings, who lovingly cleared the path for
this book to become

Ariah Cummings, who lovingly became

In Memory of
Gabrielle Bouliane 1966-2010
www.youtube.com/watch?v=gePQuE-7s8c

To Build a Swing

You carry
All the ingredients
To turn your life into a nightmare —
Don't mix them!

You have all the genius
To build a swing in your backyard
For God.

That sounds
Like a hell of a lot more fun.
Let's start laughing, drawing blueprints,
Gathering our talented friends.

I will help you
With my divine lyre and drum.

Hafiz
Will sing a thousand words
You can take into your hands,
Like golden saws,
Silver Hammers,

Polished teakwood,
Strong silk rope.

You carry all the ingredients
To turn your existence into joy

Mix them, mix
Them.

— **Hafiz,** *The Gift* (P. 48)[1]

CONTENTS

Introduction

The Three Strategies (and Why Motorcycles Matter)

I spent almost a decade working as a motorcycling instructor. It was there that I learned about and mastered the three strategies of accountability, collaboration, and initiative—strategies I further refined by my training and work as a counselor, coach, workshop facilitator and educator.

Accountability means being responsible for who you are today. You either have excuses or results. You don't blame the past for who you are, you know your strengths, and you know where you are headed. In the motorcycle-training world, accountability typically means the following:

- It's usually not the bike's fault; nine times out of ten, it's the rider.
- Decide who's in control: You ride the bike; it doesn't ride you. The motorcycle is a powerful machine, and you have the capacity to control it.
- Work with your strengths; augment your challenges with the right equipment, the right bike, and the right riders.
- Where you look is where you go. If you need to go around a pylon, but you spend all your time looking directly at it, you will hit it. Look at the intended path of travel.

Collaboration means choosing the right people to travel with you as you pursue your vision. It's about nurturing the people who nurture you. It's your community, your mentors, and your "inner circle of champions."

- You can learn on your own and fall down often. you can learn from someone who's never been there and fall down hard. Or, you can learn from a pro, fall down occasionally (it is inevitable), and get back on the seat again. Choose wisely.
- It pays to find and work with the best.

Initiative means stepping out of your comfort zone. It is aspiring to navigate the abyss between what is and what can be. It is navigating the abyss in spite of your fears.

- It means that if you're riding and looking at the cone, you're more likely to hit it. But that rule is not universal, nor does it apply when looking at pedestrians, oncoming Mack trucks, or skyscrapers as you pass them by.
- A positive mindset coupled with expert knowledge is a powerful force that can propel you forward faster than you thought possible.
- If you're going to go down, you may as well do it in the training pit.
- Determination and persistence will move you closer to taking the trip of your lifetime.

These three strategies have universal applications. For many women, learning to ride a motorcycle is a symbolic metaphor for stepping out of your comfort zone, taking calculated and measured risks, and pursuing the dream of a lifetime.

That, in short is the answer to why motorcycles matter. The rest of the book examines subsequent questions about how to become the unstoppable woman of your own quest, whether it is pursuing your life as an entrepreneur, a business person, an artist, a mother or a dreamer.

WHAT THESE THREE STRATEGIES CAN DO FOR YOU

The act of reading this book indicates that you are ready to move forward. I suspect you are a progressive growth-oriented woman who can anticipate what comes next in her life and can turn challenges into growth opportunities. You are also probably belief-based in that you take everything in stride: you have succeeded before, and you know you will again. From learning to walk to passing third grade to getting your first job, you have succeeded many times. Like all other women, you have also tasted the bitter pill of failure; your past successes were achieved either in spite of or because of those failures.

- Your past successes (and failures) have given you a certain level of experience that causes you to rise above others.
- Failures have fed you and spurned you toward success.

To become unstoppable, you must acquire a new skill set, and that skill set consists of three key cornerstone elements: accountability, collaboration and initiative.

It is now your time to conquer inner worlds and achieve great new results! With the insights presented in this book, you will learn how to:

- Strengthen your impact as a leader.
- Increase the clarity of your life purpose.
- Achieve your intended contributions.
- Intensify your influence.
- Expand your resource pool.
- Unearth your unstoppable self.
- Attain heights greater than you imagined possible.

Demanding personal conformity with an unalterable depiction of perfection is the surest path to self-destruction. This one life and one body are the most treasured gifts you've ever received. First and foremost, always remember to be kind to yourself.

Do not believe in anything simply because you have heard it.
Do not believe in anything simply because it is spoken and rumored by many.
Do not believe in anything simply because it is found written in your religious books.
Do not believe in anything merely on the authority of your teachers and elders.
Do not believe in traditions because they have been handed down for many generations.
But after observation and analysis, when you find that anything agrees with reason and is conducive to the good and benefit of one and all, then accept it and live up to it.
— Buddha (Hindu Prince Gautama Siddharta, the founder of Buddhism, 563-483 B.C.)

You are ready for growth. With growth comes change. With change comes a new level of awareness. With new levels of awareness comes the ability to solve problems and achieve remarkable results. And with the remarkable results comes your unstoppable self.

How This Book is Organized

This book is divided into three sections. Each section discusses various aspects of the three strategies: accountability, collaboration, and initiative.

Throughout this book, you will encounter Calls to Action, which invite you to contemplate and record, or to complete a list or an exercise.

Whether you take up the challenge of the Calls to Action is up to you. I won't make the claim that your completion of these Calls is critical in order for you to become unstoppable. But completing them can help, and it ultimately boils down to what you do with the information contained within this book as a whole. If exercises appeal to you, do them. If you want a more structured workbook, that too is available to you (without charge) from the website, www.thethreestrategies.com. If you don't want to do the exercises, that too is your prerogative.

The Calls to Action are there to provoke your thought process. Whether you record your thoughts is up to you.

We Are All In the Middle of Our Stories

In writing this book, I seek to remind you that we are all in the middle of our stories. Just like you, I have not yet arrived at the final destination (either death or perfection), and I really have no idea how it will all conclude. There are no end-result guarantees.

In reading this book, I invite you to be in the middle of your story. I invite you to be imperfect. I invite you not to seek a narrowly defined pinnacle of success but to nurture your experience, for through this experience you will achieve success. I invite you NOT to know. In doing so, you will find that your business life, your personal life, your family life, and your inner joy will exceed your expectations.

These are things I do know:

- The forward momentum that nurtures the unstoppable being comes from the merging and continual development of personal accountability, interpersonal relationships, and perpetual forward action.

- Forward momentum increases the likelihood of a positive outcome, although there are no guarantees.

- If you don't do anything at all, if you opt for stagnation at a place that is comfortable although not quite delightful, the likelihood of improving your current situation is little to none.

While you can't re-create the past to suit your present desires, you can change your habitual ways of being, and you can design different outcomes. You can always change the direction of your journey.

As you turn this next page, you move into your new potential—and I am honored to be included in your journey!

Section I

ACCOUNTABILITY

The Sun Never Says

Even
After
All this time
The sun never says to the earth

"You owe
Me."

Look
What happens
With a love like that,
It lights the
Whole
Sky.

— **Hafiz,** *The Gift* (P. 34)

Accountability is the first strategy. Accountability means accepting responsibility for who you are today. In accepting responsibility, you own your past, present and future:

- Past: Take ownership of what is yours to claim, and leave behind what does not belong to you.
- Present: Acknowledge, recognize, and celebrate the incredible talents that are your inevitable responsibility to own.
- Future: Move forward in life with clarity and purpose.

Who you are today is a combination of events that have happened to you AND your response to each event. Everything you have and are today can be directly attributed to decisions you have made in the past.

Ultimately, you establish your direction. Which direction are you facing? Do you choose decline, stagnation, or growth?

A woman who is accountable lives by the following guidelines:

- She takes full responsibility for herself in this moment.
- She shares the information she receives with others who can also benefit from it rather than withholding it or keeping it secret.
- She seeks feedback from others and continually seeks to improve herself.
- She has high aspirations and expectations for herself.
- She respects the people in her life.
- She does not blame others when things go wrong but rather learns what she can do to resolve or prevent both new and re-emerging issues.
- She is a straight-talker.
- She effectively communicates her expectations to all who work with her.
- She makes information transparent and accessible, in the truest sense.

Being fully accountable means taking full responsibility for both the negative and the positive outcomes in your life. You don't have to like them—you just have to own them. Let go of blame. Stop making other people responsible for your well-being. Let go of excuses.

When you own it, you can change it! When you are in control of your life, you will naturally want to improve and grow.

The next four chapters will give you key insights into your first steps toward accountability.

Chapter 1

WHAT'S YOUR EXCUSE?

The first step toward becoming accountable is to become aware of the excuses you are making about your current situation. Accountability means "The buck stops here." Excuses weaken our resolve. They remove responsibility for the outcome—whatever that outcome may be—from us and place that responsibility upon others. When we blame others, it means we have surrendered our power by letting them, not us, determine the outcome. Confidence through accountability means the ability to impact the outcome directly. As long as the finger is pointed outward, we have no accountability but also no opportunity to influence our future for the better.

Take Marianne for example. For years, Marianne could not advance in her profession. She was very good at her job as an ad copywriter; in fact, she seemed to be so good that she would not now or ever be promoted upward. She had worked for the same company for three years and then, thinking she might find more opportunity elsewhere, she made a lateral move to another company. After two years with the new company, she had still not advanced in her field. When she came to see me, she was tired of looking through the proverbial glass

> *You take your life in your own hands, and what happens?*
> *A terrible thing: no one to blame.*
> — Erica Jong

ceiling without being able to break through it. As we delved deeper into her situation, her list of excuses grew.

She assumed that her work should speak for itself and that if she earned a promotion, it would come her way. Marianne had not asked for a raise or a promotion because she felt it was beneath her to bring it up. If it were deserved, her boss should recognize that and give it to her. But no matter how hard she worked, the men in her office got promotions while she was always bypassed.

While Marianne wanted the increased status and raise that came with a promotion, she was hesitant to take on the steep learning curve of asserting herself so she could get it.

As I came to know Marianne better, she revealed to me that she had been abused as a child, which resulted in her having anxieties about asserting her rights to a man in a position of authority over her. She had experienced abuse because as a female and a child, she was an easy victim. She had been vulnerable at the wrong time and exposed to the wrong person. Ever since, she felt victimized by what she could not control. Society had failed to protect her, and now it owed her something.

As we explored her situation further, Marianne figured out that her own beliefs were what was holding her back. Because she feared and revered men, she would not assert herself. Her male counterparts were networking their way into raises while she was passively waiting for recognition. The excuses she made actually were ways for her to avoid taking responsibility for her own destiny. Yes, she was abused as a child, and yes, she was let down by a society that was unable to assist her in any meaningful way, but she used those experiences from her past as leverage so she could excuse herself from any responsibility *for the things that happened to her in the present.*

Life happens. This we know.

We have all, to some degree or another, suffered. I can easily reach into the bag that contains my past and pull out incidences of sexual violence, unemployment, poverty, and

Growing old is a privilege denied to many.
— Anonymous

despair. I'm willing to bet you can do the same. Depending on the severity of suffering, the degree to which one had or didn't have choices, the duration, and the individual's personality, you may need different degrees of assistance in order to end your suffering and to get on with your life. We also have little control over the lottery that places us in certain situations such as the country where we are born, our available opportunities, our experiences with cataclysmic events (such as tsunamis, earthquakes, mudslides, floods, and so on), the conditions of our individual cultures and the world, and last but by no means least, the families into which we are born.

Life is suffering. According to Buddhists, this is the first noble truth, an irrefutable fact that we must acknowledge. Life comes with its original blessing (existence through birth) and is met with physical and psychological pain. Our bodies will encounter aging, illness, disease, and death while our minds cling to the memory of youth. Our minds will experience angst, fear, frustration, disappointment, and anger. We'll attach ourselves to a status, only to find that when we think we have achieved our goals, the rules have changed. Or the environment changes. Or we change, and we find that what we thought we wanted, we no longer desire.

Life is also a process. The suffering we all experience is a part of that process. All that exists is eternally changing. The past is unchangeable. It is only in this very moment that you can choose to continue as you did yesterday or to stop, notice, turn around, or otherwise change direction, and try another way.

> *Becoming more aware of the mental program stored in the subconscious is the first step to personal freedom. The second step is evaluating those programs to see if they are in harmony with our goals and values and if they are effective in achieving those goals. The final step is to change the ineffective ones to practice the new behaviors.*
> — **Robert Gerzon,**
> *Finding Serenity in the Age of Anxiety*

Becoming more aware of the mental program stored in the subconscious is the first step to personal freedom.

The phrase, "victim mentality" reflects a framework or emotional template of self-pity that we use to house this state of suffering. This is also known as the "woe-is-me" syndrome, the "I feel sorry for myself" attitude. It is the beginning of martyrdom. We can easily recognize this mentality in others, but it can be hard to recognize in ourselves—especially when we shield ourselves by blaming others.

You can either have excuses or you can have results. If you genuinely want results, you must make a conscious effort to minimize your excuses. To become fully accountable for your life, you must drop debilitating excuses, become aware of your default mental programming, and reframe your understanding of self.

This first strategy will be the most difficult—as such, it is the most critical. If you cannot claim ownership to your own story, you will continue the life you have lived and chosen so far.

MOVING FROM MARTYR TO CHAMPION

In order to nurture the first strategy, accountability, we need to distance ourselves from the martyr mentality. The further we are situated *away* from martyrdom, the greater ownership we have over our own circumstances. This distance from martyrdom grants us the ability to move forward by our own volition, giving us greater control to determine our own destiny.

We are a victim-centric society; we are conditioned to live with a victim mentality. In this victim-centric state, we blame others for what's wrong with our lives and/or the rest of the world. Life just "happens to us." We let our past determine our present and our future.

For some, the key to breaking the victim mentality is contained in language. For instance, a woman may be encouraged to call herself a *rape survivor* rather than a *rape victim*. For others, the key is contained in your mindset. For instance, a woman may need to discern how a past survival tactic (such as physical disassociation) might not be an advantageous tactic in the present. External events will shape you, but your response to them will ultimately determine your experiences in life.

In this following section, we will look at four archetypes. Archetypes are information-rich categories that help us to understand the complexities of our nature and how we function.

The Martyr (I'm Wounded and Broken; You're Strong)

The Martyr suffers because she was unjustifiably damaged in her past, and now she is overwhelmed by a sense of oppression and powerlessness. She feels helpless and hopeless. She is ashamed of who she is today, and she wants a prince (metaphorically speaking) to come and save her.

I was strongly positioned as a Martyr for two long decades. After being sexually assaulted, I felt broken and as if the world owed me something. For twenty years, I waited for retribution, all the while believing that my life's destiny was limited by my socially imposed role as a subservient woman. I felt victimized, oppressed, and powerless, and I acted accordingly—what I produced reflected that state of mind. While I was waiting for the world to change to suit me, my life stagnated. I bounced from one minimum-wage job to the next, one boarding room to the next, one relationship to the next.

> We cannot have a world where everyone is a victim. "I'm this way because my father made me this way. I'm this way because my husband made me this way." Yes, we are indeed formed by traumas that happen to us. But you must take charge, you must take over, you are responsible.
> — Camille Paglia

The Rescuer (I'm Broken, but I'll Help You Get Better)

The Rescuer is often an enabler, one who allows the Martyr to perpetuate her state of misery. The Rescuer is indeed dependent on the Martyr's "stuck" state because it reinforces the Rescuer's identity or role.

I also have done my time as a Rescuer. I spent a decade working with other women in a counseling setting. I helped a fair number of women along the way, but my primary motive was to feel better about myself by "fixing" others. Although I helped other women to recover from trauma, I was not prepared to deal with my own problems.

Do you find yourself standing on the shoulders of fallen and broken people in order to boost your own sense of self? If so, it may be time to step off their shoulders and start standing by your own volition.

The Tyrant (I'm Absolutely Right; You're Absolutely Wrong)

The Tyrant is the perfectionist bully who is out to prove that the world is wrong and that she is always "right." She spends a lot of time positioning herself intellectually. Directly or indirectly, she says, "It is all your fault." She spends a lot of time feeling sorry for herself and blaming others for her miserable lot in life. She is highly critical and often mobilized to action only through anger. She is a rigid authoritarian who clearly (in her own mind) already has all the answers.

> We are not responsible for what got programmed into our subconscious; all of the important software was loaded into our brains during our first few years of life. But, as adults, we are responsible for whether or not we keep it there.
> — Robert Gerzon,
> Finding Serenity in the Age of Anxiety

She is also in a very interesting predicament. In her rigid belief that she is right, she won't attempt anything where she cannot win. If she doesn't try, she can't fail. And if she can't fail, she will continually be "successful."

In the Tyrannical state, we become exceedingly petty and poison the world with harsh judgment.

The Champion (How Can I Help You?)

Whereas the Rescuer is broken and finds a measure of value in helping others, the Champion derives her sense of purpose and value from within. As the ultimate heroine, she knows she is okay in every way, that she is in control of her destiny, and that she can achieve what she wants in life regardless of what happens to her. She seeks those who are more skilled than her so she can learn from their experiences. When she reaches out to those who are broken, it is not to find her worth, identity, or value; it is done in service to the other.

The Champion accepts that she is the creator of her destiny. She knows she can remodel whatever disaster befalls her and grow as a result of it, and she demands that same level of accountability from others.

This book will give you the tools to drive forward your own unstoppable creative self, which will in turn allow you to maximize the amount of time you spend as a Champion. Unless you liken yourself to Mother Teresa, living in the Champion paradigm 24/7 should be an aspiration not a concrete goal. As with most mortals, you will continue to experience all four of these roles, from Martyr to Champion. The objective is not to be "perfect" or to attach yourself to one particular role; it is gradually to spend more time associating with your inner Champion and less time with the other three.

MAPPING THE ARCHETYPES

Were you to map the four archetypes alongside the four quadrants of the 1969 bestseller by Thomas A. Harris, MD, *I'm OK, You're OK*, the completed chart would look like this.

1	YOU'RE OK		4
I'M NOT OK	**MARTYR** • "I'm broken" • Blameless • "Poor me" • Victimized • Oppressed • Hopeless • Helpless • Powerless • Ashamed • Seeks rescuer	**CHAMPION** • "I'm getting on with my life" • Director of own life • Gives without expectation of return • Holds self to a high standard • Holds others to a high standard	I'M OK
I'M NOT OK	**RESCUER** • "I'll save you" • Enabler • Reinforces victim mentality • Gives permission to fail • Expects to fail	**TYRANT** • "I'm right" • "It's your fault" • Blames • Criticizes • Keeps others oppressed • Mobilized by anger • Rigid • Authoritarian	I'M OK
2	YOU'RE NOT OK		3

Another model is offered by David Logan[2], a faculty member at the University of Southern California, in his work on tribal stages. Per Logan's definition, a "tribe" is a group of people defined by a set of commonalities.

Again, understand that we're dealing with categories. Categories enable a deeper understanding of the components within us. While each individual celebrates freedom of choice and a freedom of personality, we are simultaneously equally predictable.

TRIBAL STAGE	% OF PEOPLE AT THAT STAGE	DESCRIPTION	IN THE FOUR QUADRANTS	MARTYR
Life sucks	2%	Despairing hostility. Life is suffering, so I'll fully engage in that suffering. Commonly seen among prisoners and mafia members.	Martyr, as perpetrator of the crimes committed against him or herself.	
My life sucks	25%	Victim/Martyr mentality. Somebody owes me something; life should be good, but something really bad happened to me.	Martyr, as sufferer	
I'm great	48%	Lone Warrior. I'm great; you're not so great.	Rescuer: I'm great at your expense. Tyrant: I'm great; you're wrong.	
We're great	22%	Team pride. Values, recognition that the whole is bigger than the individual parts.	Champion, beginning steps. Optimum human state.	
Life is great	2%	Altruistic pursuit of a noble cause. Truth and reconciliation prevail. Example: Mother Teresa.	Enlightened Champion, free from ego connections to his or her identity; does for the sake of doing, regardless of what's in it for him or her.	CHAMPION

I compare my Four Quadrants with the works of Harris and Logan to show that we are working with types, and that types can be categorized and thus understood. However you choose to categorize it, on whatever scale, what matters is that you understand there are different ways to experience life. When blame is heightened, you're closer to one end of the spectrum; when accountability is heightened, you're closer to the other end. Through increased awareness, you can adjust your position on this scale.

Keep in mind that these categories are on a scale and are not presented with firm, indestructible parameters. When you find yourself playing the Martyr, acting as the Rescuer, or being the Tyrant, become aware of what you're doing and gently nudge yourself toward quadrant four and your image of the Champion.

CALL TO ACTION

Recall a time when you have played each of the four roles. Because recalling certain life experiences can bring up shame or self-doubt, the memories may be difficult to relive. However, beginning to admit our own role is the beginning of assuming responsibility. Responsibility begets accountability, and accountability lets you "drive your own car," "direct your own show," or whatever metaphor works best for you.

1. When have you played, or when do still play, the role of the **Victim**? Think of a specific incident. What did it feel like? What did it sound like? What did it look like? Make some notes below.

2. When have you played, or when do still play, the role of the **Rescuer**? Think of a specific incident. What did it feel like? What did it sound like? What did it look like? Again, you can make some notes below.

3. When have you played, or when do still play, the role of the **Tyrant**? Remember a specific incident. What did it feel like? What did it sound like? What did it look like? Record your thoughts.

4. When have you played, or when do still play, the role of the **Champion**? Think of a specific incident, or think about what an ultimate hero would look like to you. What does it feel like? What does it sound like? What does it look like? Write it down! This one's for YOU.

Now that you are seeing the full-range of yourself and becoming aware of your inner "higher self"—your inner and true hero—you are now ready to think like a Champion and tackle your life accordingly. In the next section, we will look at the mindset behind thinking BIG while making certain that you don't fall victim to the greatest human weakness.

THE GREATEST HUMAN WEAKNESS

Accountability is partially about claiming your own baggage. We've examined some of the unpleasant contents of that baggage. Now, let's look for some of the good stuff. It's there. I guarantee you. You've just got to reach down far enough, rummage around long enough, and recognize real treasure once you find it.

In his book *The Magic of Thinking Big*, David J. Schwartz claims that the greatest human weakness is self-deprecation.[3]

Reread that line until it really sinks in. How many times have you told yourself that your strengths really aren't all that amazing? How many times have you belittled your strengths even after someone else has told you your talent truly is remarkable?

One of my inherent qualities is delegating. When I was promoted from senior to chief instructor with the Canada Safety Council (Canada's top motorcycle safety school), I had to undergo a weekend of intensive training. One of the assignments the trainees were given was designed to push us out of our comfort zone and demonstrate to the examiner how we would solve an unsolvable problem.

The night before we were to give our presentations, while the others went to their hotel rooms to prepare, I came up with my game plan, went to the bar for a drink, and then went to bed. The next day started with the grand finale, our presentations. I sat through a multitude of awe-inspiring presentations that included flip charts, soundtracks, cross references, and overview maps. Then I was up. With clammy palms and knocking knees, I stuck to my plan—not because I was convinced my plan was great, but because I had no time to change it. I divided the group up into four teams, and re-presented the problem to them. Each team was to come up with one to three solutions. After a specific amount of allotted time went by, we returned to being one group to brainstorm for the best solution.

In the middle of my process, I glanced up at the lead examiner and was dismayed to see that he had dropped his marking pen and was not taking notes like he had with all the others. Instead, he was sitting back with his arms crossed and rocking his chair back. What could only be a smirk was on his face.

I groaned. Surely I had failed the test.

I then thought, "I'm deep into this program, and I'm not going to walk away defeated." I turned back to my group and completed the exercise. I ended my presentation as planned and then turned to the evaluators for their marks and feedback.

Brian, the lead examiner, had only two words for me. "Kobayashi Maru."

Frowning, I replied, "I have no idea what you mean."

"Look it up," he said. "You passed with flying colors."

Later, I did research that strange phrase. Kobayashi Maru refers to an episode in the television show "Star Trek," where Captain Kirk solves an unsolvable computer program by rewriting the computer program itself. Some liken this to cheating; others say it's brilliant problem-solving. I prefer the latter, of course! Brian did as well.

When Brian spoke with me later, he told me he had stopped marking because I had essentially rewritten the assignment and completed it based entirely on my rewrite. He couldn't mark me because his marking scheme was no longer applicable. He told me that in all of his years of administering chief promotions, he had never had anyone take this approach. It was by far the most creative approach he had ever seen in his years of administering the final and ultimate upgrade.

I did not value my ability to facilitate, to lead a group through a brainstorm session, and to come up with a remarkable solution. I just did what came easily to me, but because I doubted my own capabilities, my *interpretation* of the event was that I had failed. It had not been a smirk on Brian's face but a smile of amazement. He did not drop his marking pen because he was going to give me a failing grade but because I had exceeded all expectations.

Brian thought my skill to delegate the problem was genius, and this skill continues to serve me well.

If you are self-deprecating about your own talents, perhaps it's time to reevaluate your inventory of strengths and skill sets. If you hear other people saying that something you do quite easily is remarkable, and you find yourself saying, "Oh, really, it's nothing," stop and reassess the value you place on your own skills and talents.

One of my neighbors, Terri Rowe Boizard, is a mother to three beautiful children. Terri "tinkers" in photography. If you walk into her house, you'll think you are in an art gallery, surrounded by a multitude of professional photographs of her children at various stages in their lives. The photos capture her children's essence, seldom seen so up close and personal.

The photographs you see here are those of my daughter taken by Terri. On a fall day, she captured the angelic essence of my daughter, Ariah along with other children in the neighborhood. A few rolls of film resulted, with each picture as breathtakingly beautiful as the next. Terri managed to capture the angelic side of childhood that often goes unnoticed in our hectic pace of living, or lost in childish tantrums and parenting predicaments.

Her studio? The great outdoors. All she did to prepare for her photo shoot was to set up a bale of hay, call over a bunch of neighborhood kids, and begin shooting images with her trained eye and camera. The kids were to "come as they are." Parents were dissuaded from fixing wild hairdos and changing their children's clothes. She has given me permission to include a few of those photographs here.

Terri spent forty-five minutes watching the kids playing and casually taking pictures; the neighborhood parents were delighted at the gift of these incredible photos.

I have tried time to convince Terri that she has a valuable coveted skill she can turn into money, while positively serving the community.

To which she steadily replies, "It's nothing really; just something I do for fun. No one would ever pay me for that!"

Again and again, I beg to differ!

Whatever it is you are good at, from singing to painting to organizing corporations, it's a skill someone else will appreciate. If you are providing a valuable service and if *you* value your skill, then you have something of incredible value that can change your world and/or the world around you.

The Magic of Thinking Big makes it clear that each and every one of us is important and worthy of BIG aspirations. If you find yourself thinking small far too often, you can draw on one of my favorite quotes from T. Harv Eker: "Don't believe a word you think." If you generally think small and belittle yourself, there's great truth in this statement.

CALL TO ACTION

What follows is the first of many lists you will compose during your journey through this book.

1. List ten things you are reasonably good at.

2. List five things you consider to be your top strengths.

3. List three things other people consider to be your talents.

4. List three things your mother (or a mother figure in your life) most admires about you.

For each item above, make a list of skills required to be successful at that particular strength or talent.

LUCK AS A SELF-FULFILLING PROPHECY

According to Seneca, the Roman dramatist, philosopher, and politician, luck "is what happens when preparation meets opportunity." If you are closed to the possibility of opportunity, all the preparation in the world won't serve you.

Luck is a perfect example of self-fulfilling prophecy. It can be self-defined. If you believe you are lucky, you will be lucky. If you're convinced you are forever unlucky, then being unlucky is what you will experience in life.

Do you think of yourself as one of the world's lucky people? Do amazing things happen to you seemingly out of the blue? Conversely, do you see yourself as one of the world's unlucky people? Do miserable things keep happening to you?

We have recently heard much chatter about thoughts perpetrating our realities. In fact, some Law of Attraction proponents advocate that your entire reality is based on your thoughts. I don't take it that far, but I do believe that what you think is what you will see.

Consider the famous glass-half-empty scenario. It's a bit cliché, but it holds a vital kernel of truth that bears repeating.

People who consider themselves lucky, who believe that good things typically happen to them, would look at a half-full glass of water and know that they have enjoyed what they have already consumed. Not only have they enjoyed the first half of the glass, but they see an equal amount of beverage/substance/joy still ahead. The super-optimist may even go so far as to point out that she can refill her glass when it is empty. The word *abundance* comes to mind.

People who consider themselves unlucky, on the other hand, would bemoan that half of their glass of water is gone. They may have enjoyed the first half, but what remains is only a part of what it was before. And once that is consumed? Then what? That glass may never again be refilled. The scarcity mentality sets in. "This is all I have left, and I must savor it. I must guard it with my life." Indeed, the rest of the water may never be consumed from fear of losing and never regaining.

Richard Wiseman, a professor of psychology at the University of Hertfordshire, has studied the phenomenon of "luck." Among other things, he has shown how people who expect good luck might put more effort into their ventures, resulting in more success and thereby reinforcing their belief in good luck. Moreover, lucky people are more likely to look on the bright side of bad encounters. In a mental exercise describing being shot during a bank robbery, lucky people considered themselves lucky not to have been killed while unlucky people considered themselves unlucky to have been shot.

Wiseman wrote an article for the BBC titled "The Loser's Guide to Getting Lucky." In the article, he tells of a simple experiment he did. He gave all participants, who were self-defined as either lucky or unlucky, a newspaper and asked them to count the number of photographs they saw. Inside the newspaper he had placed a message that read, "Tell the experimenter you have seen this and win £250." This message took up half of the page and was printed in type that was more than two inches high. The self-defined unlucky people typically missed the ad, and—you guessed it—the self-defined lucky people typically spotted it. Wiseman's rationale was that self-defined lucky people are more relaxed and open to opportunity, seeing beyond the immediate task at hand. Self-defined unlucky people are tenser, and their anxiety disrupts their ability to notice the unexpected.

Here are Wiseman's four tips for becoming lucky:

1. Go with your gut. It's your instinct trying to tell you something. It's probably right.

2. Break with your normal routine. Try new things. Open yourself to new experiences.

3. At the end of each day, recount how many things actually worked out for you. You might be surprised! Spend a few moments each day remembering things that went well.

4. If you're going into a high-stress situation like a job interview or a presentation, spend a moment to visualize yourself as a lucky person. Tap into the self-fulfilling power of luck![4]

CALL TO ACTION

Here are a few questions to contemplate.

1. Do you consider yourself lucky or unlucky?

2. If unlucky, what needs to change in your life so you can consider yourself lucky?

3. How can you bring this change about?

4. How can you start finding luck in your story?

5. What lucky events can you expect to happen to you today? List three.

6. What lucky events have already happened to you today? List three

Chapter 2

(RE)CONSTRUCTING YOUR WORLDVIEW

In the first chapter, we examined some of the more generic excuses that commonly prevent us from taking responsibility for our lives, from being accountable. Life is suffering, the victim mentality, the power of self-deprecation and the self-fulfilling prophecy of luck.

In this second chapter, we're going to delve deeper into a worldview that is very gender specific.

Whether we like it or not, our gender places us in a context that is violent and misogynistic. As women, we are continually aware of sexual vulnerabilities, and we have a hypersensitivity to body image. It is important to acknowledge the feminine experience, the feminine context, because it is what shapes our experiences and consequently forms our daily beliefs. And it is also important to acknowledge that our experiences, too, can be viewed from another angle.

In order to become increasingly accountable, we need to recognize how our experiences impact (and shape) our beliefs. In the following pages, we're going to draw a line in the sand between what you are responsible for, and what clearly belongs to another person.

Ours Is a Violent World

Ours is indeed a violent world. Violence against women and children is rampant, so much so that it is not an anomaly but a norm. In the same way Buddhists declare that the first noble truth is that "life is suffering," I raise this issue not to bring another excuse to the table but rather to acknowledge the context that violence has in shaping our beliefs. If I am to live among lions, then I must acknowledge their presence. Denial has never helped one become more accountable. Denial has never nurtured confidence. Acknowledging our environment is critical in nurturing a continual increase in accountability.

When gender is a weapon of war and a means of social control, you know that misogyny exists on a large, large scale. The tactics are familiar to us all, ranging from comfort women to mass-rape to sexual enslavement to honor killings and genital mutilation.

We know of these things. They continually appear in the news and in documentaries. In fact, we are so inundated with these events that we cease to notice them or their importance. We give a distant nod and acknowledge what's happening, and then we go on with our own lives, thankful that we are living in such a "civilized" society.

But take a closer look. Think of two other women you know. Between you three, one of you has experienced and reported an incident of sexual violence. I'm willing to bet that another one of you is keeping a secret.

Statistics paint one picture; experience paints quite another.

I consider my background quite normal. I was born to a middle class family that was fragmented when my parents separated when I was fifteen. I had an older and a younger brother. We had a dog and a cat and a car. We owned our home. Dad worked, mom was at home with us kids. In the winter we went cross-country skiing; in the summer we went hiking. After the parental units divorced, we experienced a sharp drop in economic status. The children (all teens at the time) rebelled. Utterly normal. And here is a four-year snapshot of my life's framework growing up "normal," looking at feminine experience in the context of violence. These are the female stories I was surrounded with. Some of the stories are mine; most belong to others. Indirectly, they belong to us all.

- A pre-teen girl is repeatedly sexually fondled by her brother. He is found guilty and serves time in jail.

- A teenager is sexually abused by her father and decides to press charges against him. She reports the incident of incest to the police. In a world of he-said-she-said court cases, her father is found "not guilty" and walks away a free man. He claims she ruined his reputation.

- A teenager is gang-banged at a pit-party by so-called "friends." The event is never reported.

- A teenager is sexually pursued by her father. Not reported.

- A child is sexually solicited by her mother (a prostitute) for money. As a teenager, the child is then physically and sexually abused repeatedly in a succession of foster homes. When reported, she is removed to another where the event happens again; subsequent events are not reported.

- A teenager is raped by a stranger. Reported.

- A young woman is date-raped. Not reported.

- A young woman is sexually molested in a bar, and later gang-raped in a separate room. Not reported.

- A young woman is jumped and sexually mauled in front of a donut shop. Results unknown.

These unwanted and undesired sexual intrusions are just some of the ones I know about, have witnessed, or have personally experienced. Because people generally don't speak freely about these "shameful" acts, I suspect that much, much more has happened in the lives of the women who surround me.

The Perpetrator Needs Repair

Violence against women is real. Her susceptibility to abuse is not an anomaly; it's the norm. Again, look to your left and look to your right. Statistics *under-report* the real picture (we women under-report what happens to us).

What the reported statistics, and the anecdotal and personally experienced unreported non-statistics, say to me is that a woman's exposure to sexual violence, by virtue of her gender, is *normal*. Which begs the question, should "normal" and commonly occurring events be traumatized? Shouldn't it be the unusual and damaging behavior that gets mended?

I think it's safe to assume it is not a one-to-one ratio of perpetrator to victim. If we say that one third of the population has been abused, it doesn't mean that one-third of the population is a perpetrator of abuse. I think it's safe to assume that perpetrators tend to re-offend, or incur multiple offenses. I think it's safe to assume that while the female victim is in a *normal* state of being, it is the perpetrator who is the anomaly. And as such, it should be the *unusual*, the perpetrator, who receives the services, the counseling, and the continued support.

When a bully terrorizes others in the playground, it is the child with the anomalous behavior (the bully) whose behavior is addressed. When a scuffle breaks out in high school and a nose is broken, the one with the broken nose goes to the hospital to get it set; the one who delivered the nose-breaking punch might receive anger-management counseling. Yet somehow the rules are different in gender-violence. The woman is encouraged to receive counseling; the perpetrator is left to figure things out for himself.

We are fortunate enough to live in a society where it is topically permissible to discuss a crime against a woman without actually blaming her. A woman subjected to rape is typically not abandoned by her family and then stoned to death as a sport at the local community center. This acknowledgment that the woman is an abuse recipient and not at fault in these situations provides an opening for an understanding that is impossible in many parts of the world, but

> *We are made wise not by the recollection of our past, but by the responsibility for our future.*
> — George Bernard Shaw

potentially achievable here: we can begin to explore the possibility of "helping" the perpetrator to prevent him (or, yes, 5% of the time, "her") from offending or re-offending.

A big part of increasing your own accountability is accepting what you are responsible for, and then drawing a BIG line in the sand firmly stating where your responsibility ends, and where that of another begins.

If you experienced any degree of sexual interruption, it's your responsibility to acknowledge your past, make peace with it, and then set about to self-determine who you are going to be for today and tomorrow. But the violent imposition is solely the responsibility of the perpetrator. They are the ones who have deviated from the norm; they are the ones who require intensive repair.

GETTING OVER YOUR STORY

Many years ago, I worked as a crisis counselor at the Victoria Rape Crisis Centre. In our training, we were told that sexual assault victims often suffer night terrors, which explained why they'd light up the phones at 3:30 in the morning although in most cases the event was years old. It wasn't our job as crisis counselors to "cure" them but rather to "go into the dark pit" with them and accompany them during this difficult time. It was our job to hear their stories and to sit with them as they revisited the terror of the past anew.

It sounded sensible and sane. I knew that when people suffer the death of someone close, they just want to be able to talk about their grief and don't need to hear that they will "get over it someday." I'd had my own litany of bad experiences, and I had sometimes needed someone to come and sit with me.

After being on the crisis phone lines for about a year, I migrated to a different view. Many of the callers I had the opportunity to speak with had "suffered" sexual trauma years ago, so they had their stories down pat. Experienced counselors would forewarn the newer counselors about certain clients, those who knew their stories by heart and were addicted to a specific response (sympathy). When challenged to change their perspective or response, these callers would hang up and call at another time. Their primary objective was often to find a sympathetic counselor—one that allowed them to stay in a "stuck" state while blaming the rest of the world.

I understood them all too well, because for twenty years, I too was addicted to my own story, stuck in my own pit of perpetual self-wallowing misery.

Yes, it's true. I'm embarrassed to say that I spent a long time bemoaning my lot in life, recalling and reliving the pain, the humiliation, and the suffering. I often wondered whom I would be had I not suffered through these experiences. I felt how much more successful I *could have been* had these events never happened. I made excuses. I sought the rescuer. I believed that the world owed me something. And I suffered, reliving the memories again and again.

At age thirty-five, I finally quit the addiction of making excuses. I reduced the size of my "but." The feminist writer Camille Paglia was very instructive on this one. She holds a very controversial view about victimization, a view to which I subscribe:

> *"But" is an argument for your limitations, and when you argue for your limitations, you get to keep them.*
> — Les Brown

My Sixties attitude is, yes, go for it, take the risk, take the challenge—
if you get raped, if you get beat up in a dark alley in a street, it's
okay. That was part of the risk of freedom, that's part of what we've
demanded as women. Go with it. Pick yourself up, dust yourself off,
and go on.[5]

Note that this quote is somewhat out of context. For Paglia, sexual
"outcomes" are a result of risk, meaning that if you dress sexy, you will
attract the "sexual gaze." By doing so, you increase the level of sexuality
in a situation and thereby increase your personal risk.

I like the quote because it confirms for me that you CAN indeed pick
yourself up, dust yourself off, and get on with life! Paglia's statement also
recognizes that nothing is pathologically wrong with the victim.

Now there's a thought! I had always maintained that it was not the
victim who required post-trauma services but the perpetrator. The victim
needs immediate attention and support, but the long-term attention
should really be turned to the perpetrator so his crimes are never repeated
or inflicted upon society again.

Paglia also writes, "Rape does not destroy you forever. It's like getting
beaten up. Men get beat up all the time."[6] According to Paglia, it is the
perpetrator, not the woman, the so-called "victim," who needs "fixing."

When we were taught at the Rape Crisis Centre to "sit in the pit" with
a woman reliving her terrors, we were in fact pathologizing the "victim,"
viewing her as the abnormal one. Later, I shifted my view to one that
now said there nothing is truly nothing wrong with her. She is not dis-
eased. She may need help navigating her way through the immediacy of
her trauma, but she doesn't need to park her life there. The person who
needs specialized attention, and is least likely to receive it, is the perpetrator. Sadly, our culture is not quite ready to recognize this need. (In fact,
I remember some of the counselors-in-training having a venomous reaction *against* providing counsel to a rapist or child molester.)

A recipient of any form of violence, whether actively or passively perpetrated, needs recognition and needs to voice the experience; having said that, she does not need to wear a mantle of shame forever. Our job now is to get on with our lives.

THRIVING IN THE FACE OF VIOLENCE

Since choosing to lessen the focus on the victim of sexual assault and heighten the focus on the perpetrator, I've encountered many people who have survived—even thrived—in the face of violence. Writer David Pelzer chronicled his story of abuse in *A Child Called It*, which was one of the most horrific cases of child abuse in California's history. The most notable aspect of his writing is that in spite of his horrific past, Pelzer maintains that it's what you do about your circumstances that matters most. Today, Pelzer works primarily with teenagers, helping them to move beyond the past. He helps them to navigate *out* of their despair and to distinguish their identities as separate from the events that inflicted trauma.

John Walsh, host of television's "America's Most Wanted," lived through one of the most horrific events imaginable for any parent when his six-year old son Adam was abducted and murdered. Instead of lying down and metaphorically dying himself, Walsh radically changed how the law deals with child violence in North America. The work of Walsh and his family ultimately led to:

- The Missing Children Act in 1982, and the Missing Children's Assistance Act in 1984.
- The Adam Walsh Child Resource Center.
- The creation of a national sex offender registry and online tracking capabilities.
- The incorporation of the "Adam code" in many malls and department stores, where a public announcement is made when a child is either missing or found.

In October 2008, Walsh was awarded the Operation Kids 2008 Lifetime Achievement Award for his dedication to child safety.

Many sexual assault survivors have thrived despite their past. Pelzer and Walsh serve as shining examples of thriving in the face of adversity.

If you've experienced sexual abuse (or coined in my favorite way, sexual interruption), you are keeping company with some extraordinary people, including poets (Ann Sexton), singers (Sinead O'Connor, Tori Amos) and royalty (Queen Elizabeth I). Many more examples are around you, famous and not. You may not know that some of the strongest and most successful people in your life have lived through trauma. You don't realize it because *they are not their trauma*, just like you are not yours.

Women don't deserve violence. We don't invite it. It is a terrible fact of life, but whether we sink into it, sit beside it, or soar in spite of it is individually up to each of us.

YOU ARE NOT YOUR BODY

In reading *Don't Give It Away!* by Iyanla Vanzant, one particular paragraph in the section titled "Mirror Mirror In My Mind, Who Am I?" struck me:

> I have a face.
> I am not my face!
> My face is a gift that I appreciate.
> My face is not the real me.[7]

If we can all benefit from one lesson, it is the constant reminder that while we have a face, we are not that face. While we have a body, we are not that body. (The ultimate irony of course is that we talk from our *inside self*—from our brain through our body, without seeing our own face/body—to the *outside other*.)

Every day, our culture tells us otherwise. The message that "how you look" becomes "who you are" is emblazoned in the ads in the morning paper, on billboards, in the mad inundation of Internet ads, in television commercials and glossy magazines. I recently saw an ad that definitively stated that physical beauty is confidence! The brazen call to re-fashion our figures for social approval is so prevalent that we almost don't notice it anymore. It enters through our eyes, passes through the conscious mind, and parks in the subconscious mind, where it leaks into our thoughts and actions day-by-day, moment by moment.

When I was a (distressed) teenager, I remember scrutinizing my face in the mirror, hating it every time I looked at it. My nose was too big, my mouth unglamorous. I had no dimples, and my cheeks were just plain fat when I smiled. My flawed face was framed by this unruly, frizzy mass of hair I simply couldn't do anything with. In the age of Farrah Fawcett hairstyles and glamour, my look was a disaster.

One day, I confronted the demon of my appearance. I took a mirror into my room and stared at my own ugly face for about an hour. In that hour, my face began to transform. The more I sat and stared at it, the more it became detached from me. The more separate it became, the more beautiful it appeared. At the end of the process, I had achieved a complete separation from my face, from my looks. What I gazed upon was truly beautiful *when I no longer judged it as my own.*

Unfortunately, that state did not last forever. I still wanted a smaller nose, dimples when I smiled, and a flawless canvass upon which makeup would flow. From that point forward, however, I consciously was able to look at my face and separate it from my identity.

This same experience of separation has to happen with our bodies. Every human body is a miraculous entity. Considering that our anatomical origins come from the continual splitting of just one cell (our own "big bang" creation from just one cell), every human life is a miracle.

In one sense, we absolutely know we are not our bodies. When we lose a strand of hair or clip a fingernail, we do not bemoan the death of a part of ourselves. When we donate a living organ, we don't mourn our holistic depletion. When we lose a limb to cancer or diabetes, our understanding of our "self" is not eroded, although we are given new challenges in life.

On a more practical level, consider social interactions. When we are asked for our identities at a social gathering, we do not present our "packaged" selves. We do not show visitors through the rooms of our mental house. We do not say that we are blood and bones and guts, or that we are composed of angst and fears and hopes and dreams. Instead, we identify ourselves with what we *do*—we say, "I am a Web designer" or "I am a systems analyst" or "I am the president of a company" or "I am a mother of three." We write epitaphs that recall our achievements, not our appearance or obsession with it.

Some women anchor tragedy in their bodies and, in that way, define themselves as their bodies. Our bodies may have been damaged by rape, by violence, by unimaginable hurts. Our bodies are damaged by images of flaws—our thighs are too wiggly, our hips too wide, our ankles too thick.

We live in a world that simultaneously worships and despises the female body. We uphold an image of feminine perfection and despise anything that doesn't fit the cultural mythology. Only a miniscule percentage of the female population fits the physical image presented in the media; this amounts to an enormous amount of self-hatred.

I was recently invited to a Halloween party whose theme was the '80s, an era when bodies were shameless sexy and shamelessly flaunted.

What interested me was my own reaction to the costumes. My first visual intake was dedicated to the women. I immediately looked to match their costumes to their body-types. One skinny suburban mother was dressed in skin-clinging clothes. The other sleek neighbors were physically adorned as Madonna and Alice Cooper (yes, she went as "he"). Yet another slightly more Rubenesque suburban mom had chosen to mimic the gender-obscured Boy George by wearing much looser-fitting clothes. My attention was immediately drawn to how each woman dressed her body and how her figure was either pronounced or obscured, depending on her physique and the corresponding costume.

My observation of the men was completely different. Three middle-aged suburban men (of varying physiques) dressed as members of the band Kiss drew my attention. First, I took in their platform boots, white-painted faces, and big hair. Then I noticed their air guitar playing and gestures, and I was taken in by their playful, silly, and full-on antics.

Eventually, after about an hour or so, I noticed how their costumes adorned their bodies. Their spandex suits left nothing to the imagination. That they were over thirty-five was obvious. Their flesh was a little softer and a bit more bulbous than it might have been in the past.

In that moment of noticing my own observation of others, it dawned on me that men don't measure each other on their physical appearance— or at least not in a personal-identification kind of way. The ease with which these men existed in their bodies, their state of complete liberty with their soft bellies hanging over the edges of their belts, and their incredibly easy and nonjudgmental interaction with each other amazed me. Based on my own observations, I realized that I was less inclined even to consider their bodies. Noticing their bodies was the last thing I noticed, whereas with the women, it was first.

This revelation is not new but as old as the ages. In the Renaissance, the godly man was associated with the divinity of his mind; the woman, the "leaky vessel," was anchored through her body to the earth.

It is not just a difference of whether we first notice the mind or the body. Consider that the power of the mind, the intellect, is determined on a continuum. A range of "smartness" exists, regardless of what measuring instrument you want to use. The power of physical beauty, however, is derived from what is "average." The "average hypothesis" asserts that our eye is attracted to the person who represents the average physical image of ourselves. The eye distance, the size of the nose, the lips, and the chin are all components of this average. As the point of average, it's very exact. Because the average represents an ideal, not an actual person, it is largely unattainable for the bulk of the population—99% approximately.

The average standard of beauty is then convoluted with a mass-marketing formula: Identify an area with which women are dissatisfied (and if it doesn't exist, create it) and then sell a product that promises to resolve that dissatisfaction. Marketing is why we literally buy into the notion that a perfume will cause a strange man to run after us with flowers for reasons unknown even to him, or that a certain shade of lipstick makes a meal with our date taste so much better.

From the diet fads to fashion, from lipstick to vacation resorts, the invented dissatisfaction with our bodies generates billions of dollars every year.

We need an hour-long stare into the mirror where we look at our unadorned bodies until a separation occurs. We need to look until we recognize that our bodies are not ourselves. The body is a miraculous gift that each of us has been blessed with regardless of the hardships it has or may encounter. The body is a working miracle of cells and energy. The body is our vehicle to interact with the world, to bear our message and our gifts to others.

The separation needs to occur especially in women. Whatever shape or form we live in, the body is miraculous. It is time to stop judging others and ourselves by the body's outer shell.

The advertisers are not about to change this situation. We must take it upon ourselves to readdress our beliefs, our worldview, and our relationship with our bodies.

BIOLOGICALLY SPEAKING

Consider this amazing fact: the body that once was you is no longer you. Since you were conceived, your physical body has gone through so many cell deaths and growths that the physical "you" of a decade ago no longer exists.

Scientists theorize that the cells in our bodies regenerate every seven years. We know that most cell and tissue types in the human body are much younger than the person's chronological age and that very few cells live for the person's entire lifespan. The cells that don't die (and don't stop reproducing) are actually cancer cells.

Think about what this means! In my case, almost every cell in my body has been replaced since the era of my trauma, but my brain holds onto the memories for decades! If your trauma happened in your childhood, the body that was impacted no longer exists at the biological level.

If the body is able to regenerate itself and dispose of old cells, how can we help the mind to dispose of old habits of thought? Daniel G. Amen, M.D. attributes repetitive worry to the cingulated system, which is located in the brain's frontal lobe and speaks specifically to holding onto or getting "stuck" in past hurts.[8] His recommendations for getting "unstuck" include the following:

- Become aware.

- Notice when you are stuck. Step away from those stuck thoughts and come back to them later. Do not try to speak "sensibly" to anyone who is stuck, including yourself. Just notice what's going on.

- Notice what your automatic response has been and consider doing the opposite.

- Write it out. Describe the item or thought with which you are stuck as well as options and solutions.

- Seek external input. Have you ever been able clearly to see a problem (and its solution) in someone else's life even though she or he has been blind to the issue? Others may have insights that you have overlooked.

- Know what you can change and accept what you can't.[9]

Some use the acronym TLC, which stands for "Take it, Leave it, or Change it." These truly are your three core choices.

CALL TO ACTION

What story have you been hanging onto? What childhood trauma, separation, or death impacted you so significantly that you have allowed it to impede your success?

Be honest with yourself. You are writing for your life now, so evaluate the events of your life with courage.

1. What's your story? What loss have you suffered? What is your biggest source of pain? What price have you paid? How does your story impact you negatively on a daily or continual basis?

2. Reverse your thinking. What have you gained through that loss or pain? How has it served or benefited you?

3. What is one thing you can do differently today (that you haven't done yet) as a result of your story?

How Our Unspoken Signals Influence Our Reality

Projecting "victim" alerts the perpetrator.

Consider this first scenario.

A woman is walking through a parking lot at night, headed to her car. Only three cars are left in the dimly lit lot. It's dark and cold. Her footsteps echo as her heels click on the concrete floor. Halfway to her car, she hears footsteps behind her. She puts her head down and keeps her gaze locked on the next three feet of pavement ahead. Making sure that the key in her hand is obvious, she pulls her jacket closer and dashes to the car.

Now consider this scenario.

In the same situation, the woman hears footsteps approaching behind her. She turns around to locate the source. She sees a man walking in the same direction. She nods hello and keeps walking steadily toward her car. She casually turns as if hearing another sound and waves *Hello* to an unseen person in the distance.

In which scenario is the woman more likely to be assaulted?

If you selected the first, you are right. Perpetrators of stranger-assaults, as rare as they are, look for certain qualities in a victim, including fear. They will seek victims who look scared, avoid eye contact, and appear vulnerable.

Although a woman may not consciously attract violence, the signals she projects will determine whether she is more likely to become a victim.

In *that* sense, victims can, through their behavior or body language, become a magnet for a certain outcome. Having said that, let me also say that they do *not* deserve or *consciously will upon themselves* these externally inflicted traumatic experiences. By virtue of being in the wrong environment at the wrong time, you can become a casualty of the environment (e.g. a child who is taken by a child molester or a prostitute approached by a serial killer).

> It's not what happens to you; it's what you do about it that makes the difference.
> — W. Mitchell, motivational speaker

This book is not about curing the world's ills but about understanding what you can and cannot control and realizing that *no matter the event*, you always have a choice in how you respond, from the thoughts you have to the actions you take.

The question of whether or not we attract violence into our lives is complicated, to say the least. Various degrees of vulnerability are presented by our gender, religion, geographical location, and the conflicts into which we are born. A deeper awareness of what you project as well as an understanding of your standard responses to (re-occurring) events can significantly influence outcomes.

THE EVENTS THAT FORM YOUR BELIEFS

How a woman acts while she's alone in an empty parking lot will largely depend on her beliefs. If she inherently believes she is safe, she may behave one way; if she inherently believes she is in danger, she may behave another. Her beliefs may have been shaped by events in her life and are reinforced by mindset, by the re-occurring thoughts she perceives to be real.

Various experts in the contemporary field of mindset break down how thoughts and beliefs affect us in a variety of ways. Three contemporary authors who have written in depth about mindset are Anthony Robbins, Jack Canfield, and T. Harv Eker.

In his book *Unlimited Power,* Anthony Robbins states that beliefs come from a variety of sources:

- The environment in which you were raised and the environment in which you live/work/function.
- The small or significant events that have happened to you.
- The knowledge you have acquired over your lifetime.
- What you have achieved to date.
- The ability to see yourself in the future, living "as if" what you dream has already come true.[10]

In *The Success Principles*, Jack Canfield presents an even more simple formula for living the life you desire: E (Event) + R (your Response) = O (your Outcome).[11] In other words, what happens to you, in necessary combination with your response, produces a certain outcome. This is why many people can experience the same event and each have a uniquely different result.

The system used by T. Harv Eker is T → F → A → R (Thoughts lead to Feelings lead to Actions Lead to Results).[12] Unlike the previous two, Eker proposes a model that is entirely self-driven: the starting place of any result begins with your thoughts. Canfield and Robbins include external events in their formulas.

	Anthony Robbins	Jack Canfield	T. Harv Ecker
External impositions, "The world"	Environment		
	Event	Event	
Internal beliefs, "You," "Life as you know it"	Knowledge	+	Thoughts (lead to)
	Past results	Response	Feelings (lead to)
	Experiencing results in advance	=	Actions (lead to)
Your reality	Your potential	"Outcome"	"Results"

What these three authors (and countless others) are saying is that your perception of your experiences ultimately determines what you believe to be true, which in turn, forms your identity. Your story consists, at its bare-bones level, of two main influences: the external world and the internal world.

UNDERSTANDING CAUSE AND EFFECT THROUGH THE ATTRIBUTION THEORY

"Cause and effect" refers to the relationship between an event and the consequences that follow as a direct result. The Attribution Theory of psychology is a type of causality relationship that individuals use to explain or justify their behaviors. It presupposes that people attribute the outcomes of their lives to either internal or external events.

- "External" aligns causality with the outside world (for example, the weather).

- "Internal" aligns causality to attributes within the person, such as education, intelligence, and experience.

External life-shaping events include the person's past and present environments and events (whether good or bad) over a lifetime.

For instance, you may have been raised in a low-income neighborhood. If your story is that your economic situation in childhood predetermines an adult destiny of continued financial instability, you hold yourself back from success. If your story is that your childhood abuse predetermines your destiny (as either a victim or a perpetrator), then you live within that self-imposed paradigm.

Who decides how you will live as an adult in spite of (or because of) your childhood? YOU! Good or bad? You decide. Your **internal** character ultimately shapes how you respond to **external** forces, and therefore, you have a significant role in determining the person you become.

> *What is history but a fable agreed upon?*
> — Napoleon Bonaparte

When you are stuck in the victim (Martyr) mentality, you are powerless. You believe that life sucks because of what has happened in your past. Once you accept that an event's outcome is based on your response to it, you become powerful. You are able to shape your own outcomes and your own destiny.

KNOWING YOUR CORE BELIEFS

In *The End of Faith*, Sam Harris writes a "belief is a lever that, once pulled, moves almost everything in a person's life....Your beliefs define your vision of the world; they dictate your behavior; they determine your emotional responses to other human beings."[13]

Our beliefs are what keep us functioning when we go on "autopilot" which, depending on whom you listen to, is anywhere from 80% to 98% of the time. Robert Gerzon, author of *Finding Serenity in the Age of Anxiety*, writes that our inner talk "doesn't represent reality, but only our past conditioning about reality."[14]

In his workshops, T. Harv Eker talks about your money blueprint, or your beliefs about money. What you believe about money will shape your financial success. Garret Gunderson, award-winning entrepreneur, author, and teacher, proposes that wealth is a vehicle that affords you a greater ability to pursue your definite major purpose, thereby making the world a better place for everyone. According to these gentlemen, your view of—and relationship with—money hinges upon your underlying beliefs. I'd broaden that beyond "money" and say that your underlying beliefs lay the groundwork for your relationship with success.

Your "everyday beliefs" are driven by your core beliefs. Core beliefs are the strong beliefs that you hold about yourself and your world, and those beliefs influence how you think and feel.

> *Whether you think you can or whether you think you can't, you're right!*
> — Henry Ford

If you believe you are a literary artist, you will set out to accomplish becoming one. If you have an inherent belief that all writers are poor, you will drive yourself toward poverty. If you believe poets and fiction writers need to suffer or become alcoholics to produce genius, you can steer yourself toward alcoholism.

Five key elements shape your core beliefs:

- Environment (shapes your external circumstance)
- Events (shape your external circumstance)
- Education (shapes your internal perspective)
- Experience (shapes your internal response)
- Emulation (existing "as if" shapes your internal realm of possibility)

The first two are about what you receive (the passive and external influences in your life), and the last three refer to how you respond (the active and internal ingredients that you add, modify, and shape).

Ultimately, your perspective will encase everything that shapes these core beliefs.

Environment

The environment in which you grew up will impact how you see the world. It does NOT define, but it shapes your perspective. For instance, a part of my formative teenage years were spent in a poorer part of town. My parents had separated and my mother found herself burdened with the singular task of raising three teenagers, two of whom were exceedingly rebellious. We moved into an affordable townhouse in the east end of Ottawa. Because what Mom could afford was also what was affordable to other broken families, we found ourselves in an environment where the kids played rougher than other suburban kids.

My older brother had escaped to a university by this time, so he was able to re-invent himself far away from home. I still had a few years of high school to go and was eager to enjoy my newfound, freedom-from-father liberty. My dropping out of school was imminent. My younger brother and I took up with individuals who spent their pent-up frustrations on smalltime crimes such as breaking and entering, auto theft for purposes of joy riding, dealing in marijuana and hash, and drinking to the point of oblivion at outdoor pit parties. An extreme feeling of entitlement was held by my peers at the time. "Society" was a ghastly entity and boy-oh-boy did it owe us big time! It wasn't our fault we had been born into this unfair world.

This environment shaped me in the years to come. I developed a belief system that I was less deserving than others because I was damaged, poor, and angry (as were the rest of my peers at the time). I believed I was up against an uncooperative world, which included the entire justice system. Although I had a very keen sense of entitlement, I knew professional success and money would absolutely never come my way.

Events

As I mentioned earlier, bad things happen. And bad things happen to good people. And good people do not deserve or "attract" these events.

In *Man's Search for Meaning*, Victor Frankl chronicled the horrors of living as a Jewish prisoner in Nazi concentration camps during World War II. He wrote that "Even the helpless victim of a hopeless situation, facing a fate he cannot change, may rise above himself, may grow beyond himself, and by doing so change himself."[15] Frankl went on to publish more than thirty books and is most notable as the founder of logotherapy. He lectured and taught seminars all over the world and received twenty-nine honorary doctorate degrees.

Each event influences your worldview in some shape or form. Even though events influence and shape us, we must ultimately choose our mindset and path.

Education

Education is more than what you receive in the form of formal schooling. As the expression goes, there is also the school of hard knocks. The many teachers in your life include your parents, peers, and your own children. Your colleagues, supporters, and opponents are also teachers. You learn at your places of employment, your places of social engagement, and your places of leisure.

School is the most identifiable source of your education. Think of your own school years. What are you most inclined to remember? Your lessons? Your grades? Your peers? Your teachers?

My grade school teacher, Mr. D, had an affinity for young boys, and he often had his handpicked favorites. While the other classmates envied these favorites, those boys endured a living hell of their own. I remember watching Mr. D sitting at his desk with one of the boys in my class sitting on his lap. In the sixth grade (or any other grade for that matter), this behavior was highly inappropriate. We'd also hear of private after-school visits to Mr. D's home, and looking back I highly suspect some form of abuse occurred. (Mr. D committed suicide a few years later.) The formative years of these young boys in the educational system undoubtedly shaped their internal responses to external input.

On the other hand, I was lucky to know a great principal, Mr. Turner. Although I was a chronic outsider and constantly picked on by my peers, Mr. Turner recognized a spark in me and made me the class valedictorian for my eighth-grade graduation. I didn't know at the time that this honor was typically reserved for the most popular girl judged most likely to succeed by her peers.

I received a different form of education as a high school dropout, and yet another form of education three years later when I took the steps to go back to school and get into university.

The education I received taught me a great deal about justice, empathy, and compassion. It taught me about life on the streets, and it taught me that there are always back alleys that lead out. It taught me self-reliance and the importance of leveraging resources.

Everything you have learned and have accomplished has contributed to your education, your degree in Life.

Experience

Your past experience will shape what you believe about the present. If you set out on the path of an entrepreneur and fail, you may decide that all business ventures are inclined to fail. If you invest outside of your comfort zone and the world economy then takes a nose-dive, you may never venture into the investment arena again.

If you used to climb trees to pick and eat the delicious apples growing in the field behind your house, you'll probably be inclined to help your children learn to climb trees. If, on the other hand, that same scenario caused you to fall and break your arm, you might be less inclined to encourage your children to tree-climb.

While your past experiences influence your current preferences, they need not define you. Some experiences will serve you well throughout your life; others, although they may have served you well in the past, are no longer helpful. It's up to you to discern which is which and change what you can.

Emulation

Emulation is a modeling technique drawn from Neurolinguistic Programming (NLP) in which you walk the walk and talk the talk of the person who has achieved your desired goal. By emulating that person's behavior, you can adopt his or her neurology and thought patterns—and achieve the same level of success.

You create your future as you become that entity.

How we dress influences how we live "as if." Why do you think businesses have dress codes? If the employees dress the part, they are more likely to become consummate professionals.

You can shape your future by beginning, today, to act the part of the person you want to become.

Knowing the Power of Your Thoughts

Perspective

In the nineteenth century, John Godfrey Saxe (1816-1887) wrote the poem "The Blindmen and the Elephant" (see next page). In it, six blind men approach an elephant and stand beside it. Each man shares his experience. Of course, his experience depends entirely on where he is positioned. Each man erroneously assumes that his experience is the definitive truth, neglecting its relevance to his positioning—his particular perspective—that determines his experience. The first likens the elephant to a wall, the second to a spear, the third to a snake, the fourth to a tree, the fifth to a fan, and the sixth to a rope. Ultimately, the "truth" remains the same; what differs is where each man is positioned, i.e. his perspective.

As our perspective sets the compass for our experiences, we define our reality. Through the repetition of acts like our daily routines, we further ingrain our interpretations of reality. Every day we "touch the elephant" at the same spot. We drive the same route to work. We order similar things at the same restaurants. Our interpretations are also shaped by events that have a strong and deep emotional impact.

Robert Gerzon writes about how the past influences our responses, why we keep repeating ineffective ones, and what we can do to promote effective responses.

[P]ast experiences influence us today because they have become stored in our subconscious as mental programming. Ineffective programs are repeated because we are not fully aware of their

THE BLINDMEN AND THE ELEPHANT
BY JOHN GODFREY SAXE

It was six men of Hindustan
To learning much inclined,
Who went to see the Elephant
(Though all of them were blind)
That each by observation
Might satisfy the mind.

The first approached the Elephant
And happening to fall
Against his broad and sturdy side
At once began to bawl:
"Bless me, it seems the Elephant
Is very like a wall."

The second, feeling of his tusk,
Cried, "Ho! What have we here
So very round and smooth and
     sharp?
To me 'tis mighty clear
This wonder of an Elephant
Is very like a spear."

The third approached the animal,
And happening to take
The squirming trunk within his
     hands,
Then boldly up and spake:
"I see," quoth he, "the Elephant
Is very like a snake."

The Fourth reached out an eager
     hand,
And felt about the knee.
"What most this wondrous beast
     is like
Is mighty plain," quoth he;
"'Tis clear enough the Elephant
Is very like a tree!"

The Fifth, who chanced to touch
     the ear,
Said: "E'en the blindest man
Can tell what this resembles most;
Deny the fact who can,
This marvel of an Elephant
Is very like a fan!"

The Sixth no sooner had begun
About the beast to grope,
Than, seizing on the swinging tail
That fell within his scope,
"I see," quoth he, "the Elephant
Is very like a rope!"

And so these men of Hindustan
Disputed loud and long,
Each in his own opinion
Exceeding stiff and strong,
Though each was partly in the
     right
And all were in the wrong.

So oft in theologic wars,
The disputants, I ween,
Rail on in utter ignorance
Of what each other mean,
And prate about an Elephant
Not one of them has seen!

existence; they operate below the level of our conscious awareness in the unconscious mind ("you can't stop doing what you're doing until you know what you're doing"). By bringing in these old habits and mindsets to awareness and learning techniques that enable us to reprogram the subconscious, we can change our behavior.[16]

This counter-productive mental programming manifests as Automatic Negative Thoughts (ANTs).

Automatic Negative Thinking (ANTs)

In his book *Change Your Brain, Change Your Life*, Daniel Amen gives an overview of ANTs:

1. "Always" thinking. Universalizing or generalizing your interpretations of the world. "She is always grumpy." "That fax machine has never worked." Common triggers are words like always, never, no one, everyone, every time, and everything.

2. RED ANT: Focusing on the negative. Seeing only the bad in a situation. The glass is half-empty and will *never* be full again.

3. RED ANT: Fortune telling. Predicting the worst possible outcome to a situation. "If I go on this airplane, I know it will crash. Look, there's a man praying. He has an inside scoop and knows that this will happen."

4. RED ANT: Mind reading. Believing that you know what another person is thinking, even though she hasn't told you. "She's mad at me because I looked away while she was speaking."

5. Thinking with your feelings. Believing negative feelings without questioning them. "I'm lousy at writing/singing/speaking/painting/playing the piano."

6. Guilt beatings. Words like "should," "must," "ought" and "have to." SHOULDING on yourself.

7. Labeling. Attaching a negative label to yourself or to someone else. "Oh, *I see*, she's a LAWYER" (As if the professional label encompasses everything there is to know about that person).

8. Personalization. Innocuous events taken to have personal meaning. "Great, this traffic jam happened just to guarantee that I'll be late for the meeting."

9. <u>RED ANT</u>: Blame. Blaming others for your own problems. "I can't start my job because Samantha didn't finish hers." [17]

The "RED ANTs" are the more damaging ones, and the most insipid red ANT is blame.

We are a society of chronic negative thinkers. When was the last time you went an entire day without complaining? Complaint is so prevalent that a minister by the name of Will Bowen created Complaint Free Bracelets (every time you complain about something, you move the bracelet from one wrist to the other. The objective is to go for twenty-one days with the bracelet on the same wrist). Currently, six million bracelets are worn on wrists worldwide, working to change our negativity!

> *"Your thoughts create your world and your words indicate your thoughts. When you eliminate complaining from your life you will enjoy happier relationships, better health and greater prosperity. This simple program helps you set a trap for your own negativity and redirect your mind towards a more positive and rewarding life."*
> — **www.complaint freeworld.biz**

Complaining is not to be confused with correcting. In *A New Earth*, Eckhart Tolle clarifies: "[T]o refrain from complaining doesn't necessarily mean putting up with bad quality or behavior. There is no ego in telling the waiter your soup is cold and needs to be heated up—if you stick to the facts, which are always neutral. 'How dare you serve me cold soup…?' That's complaining."[18]

OVERCOMING MENTALITY OF ENTITLEMENT (ME) THINKING

Do you want to create misery for yourself? You can sink yourself into the mire of your own suffering by surrendering yourself to the Mentality of Entitlement—or ME—thinking.

ME thinking happens when you believe something is inherently owed to you.

Jane and Lucille both worked at a company I'll call "Design for Life." Both women worked in the IT division, designing employee-focused communications on the Intranet. Jane was relatively new, with just over one year of experience; Lucille had been with the organization for eight years, the last five in this particular division.

The company was an exceedingly large organization that had been unionized for years. Hit hard by the "recession" (let's face it, it was a depression) of 2008-2009, this large company underwent restructuring (or "right" sizing) in order to survive. According to union rules, employees with three years of union membership had established their worth. These employees were safeguarded against layoff. Those with less than three years would be the first to go.

Within their department, Jane was still considered a newcomer; Lucille knew the ropes. Jane's productivity was high, and she was a solution-oriented problem-solver. Clients loved working with her because they knew they could present their drafts' intent and objectives, and leave it to Jane to turn out a top class document. Lucille, on the other hand, worked to produce the bare minimum. She hated her job and took hour-long coffee breaks ("But only once a day" she would justify). Lucille managed her personal email, updated her Facebook status, and tweeted about her upcoming vacation during working hours. "Necessary recharging," she called it, "if I'm to be my most creative, they have to let me take mental breaks throughout the day." Every fifteen minutes, it seemed.

The differences between these two women came to a head at a union meeting, where the upcoming downsizing was on the agenda. Jane knew her productivity was more than double that of Lucille's, and that clients preferred being assigned to her rather than her colleague. She also knew that because she lacked the required three years union membership, her job was on the chopping block. She posed a question at the union meeting, asking why it was that productivity, results, and client-satisfaction were not a consideration for job security.

A silence filled the room, like the calm before the storm. And then the venom hit. "Three years of union membership is direct proof of productivity," she was told in no uncertain terms—and not nearly so nicely. She quietly left the meeting and within a week accepted the departure package.

In her unemployment, Jane took advantage of entrepreneurship training and is now running her own very successful editing company. Last she knew, Lucille was still working for the same employer, the same department, and still barely producing her minimum output.

Lucille, like many others, became lethargic in terms of her productivity and output. Hitting the magic number of three years with this particular organization assured her employment for life. Lucille then believed she was entitled to her title, her paycheck, and her benefits. Her productivity was no longer tied to her work, her self-esteem, or her bank account. She continues today to hate her job, hate herself, and hate her employer while committing the next twenty years to a nice tidy retirement fund that she believes her company owes her.

ME thinking goes hand-in-hand with blame, and both severely hamper anyone's ability to succeed because they place people in a position where they cease to be accountable for their output or their results in life.

CALL TO ACTION

It's time to look at your own thoughts of entitlement. We all have them. Moving beyond them starts with awareness.

1. Have you ever experienced ME thinking? Do you still? When is it triggered?

2. Who do you feel "owes" you something?

3. What can you do yourself to take control of the situation, while acting within the boundaries of your ethics?

Chapter 4

ACHIEVING CLARITY

So far, we have looked at increasing accountability by acknowledging your standard excuses and rewriting them, acknowledging your worldview and rebuilding it, and accepting that you do indeed have an inner genius you should celebrate. The final measure of full accountability is achieved through clarity. When we talk about achieving clarity, we talk about knowing exactly how you will define your success.

Success in its broadest meaning is not limited to monetary and material possessions. Success unveils abundance in countless forms in both your life and the natural world that surrounds you. Consider, for example, change. Change of all kinds invites growth. Sometimes we embrace change, but more often than not, we resist it.

DEFINING YOUR DESTINATION

The final part of maximizing personal accountability is about knowing exactly where it is you want to go.

This section is about having a purpose, a reason, and a direction in which to travel.

Goals are not the same as a life purpose. Our life purpose is the organizing principle of our existence, and if our goals are ends in themselves they become dead ends....[O]ur goals must be connected to—and organized to serve—a greater life purpose.[27]

Now that you have identified some of your top excuses and can work to eliminate them, you understand your role as creator of your life, and you have identified your inherent skills, talents, and your inner genius, so it's time to start getting a clear picture of where you want to go. What exactly do you wish to achieve in this life?

We get fixated on finding the RIGHT purpose. I've heard some life coaches use a navigational analogy, describing how a few initial degrees "off course" can result in finding yourself thousands of miles "off course" later on. This analogy assumes, however, that people travel in straight lines. Glancing into your past, have you *ever* traveled in a straight line? Even when you walk to a friend's house, you need to walk the curves and take the turns accordingly and smoothly.

Consider the process of climbing a mountain. I love the metaphor of mountain climbing because as with life, when we stop to rest and look back, we get the best view of how far we've come. Once you distance yourself from living in the past and clinging to where you came from, you can see your past in the context of the larger picture—as an event in the past becomes less significant, you are able to readjust your lenses to focus on what's truly important to you—what you want for your future. Once revitalized, you can continue your quest onward and upward.

To climb *a* mountain, you first need to identity *the* mountain. That is the specific detail you absolutely need, the clarity. Then you get your gear, you set up your training plan, you build the team, you book the flight and tour guides, and you begin your campaign. You just have to start with a direction, a desire.

Whatever path you are on right now, you must have the end in mind.

According to Stephen Covey, author of *The Seven Habits of Highly Effective People*, this is habit number two: "Begin with the end in mind."[29]

> *Ring the bells that still can ring*
> *Forget your perfect offering*
> *There is a crack, a crack in*
> *everything*
> *That's how the light gets in.*
> — Leonard Cohen's
> "Anthem"

With the general end in mind, you can begin your journey, and as you travel, your destination will become increasingly clear. You need to be okay *not knowing* exactly what the final destination will look like. You can imagine it, visualize it, and dream it. But until you actually arrive, until you land at your desired destination, you'll be traveling blindly. It is only when you have attained that goal, when you reach the top of that mountain, that you will see the view and the new landscape will open up ahead of you. Then you will set a new goal and climb the next mountain.

Don't worry about finding the "right" life's purpose. Be gentle with yourself. Once you are in motion, you will discover the specifics. While you may have anticipated some of them, others will come as a complete surprise. Know what you are about, what you stand for, what moves you, what propels you forward, what gets you out of bed in the morning, and what you want to achieve. Know what sets you in motion because it will clarify your purpose.

Start with the short-term in mind. Trying to discover the ultimate meaning to which you will tie the rest of your life is daunting to say the least.

Consider the following analogy of a road trip. Say that you value family relationship above all else, and you are committed to staying connected with your family in spite of the geography that separates you. You get an invitation to Auntie Mim's for the family reunion, and you know you wouldn't miss it for the world. You know she lives in the prairies and you have her address on a piece of paper. Although you haven't seen her house before, you trust it will be there.

> *One day Alice came to a*
> *fork in the road and saw*
> *a Cheshire cat in a tree.*
> *"Which road do I take?"*
> *she asked.*
> *"Where do you want to*
> *go?" was his response.*
> *"I don't know," Alice*
> *answered.*
> *"Then," said the cat, "it*
> *doesn't matter."*
> — Lewis Carroll
> (1832-1898)

As you set out for the four-day drive, you start to visit the pending reunion in your mind. You recall relatives you haven't thought of in years. You begin being "there" although you are still "here" in your mind.

You don't know where you will sleep each night. You will drive as far as you can each day and wherever you land you trust there will be a motel. Incidents crop up along the way—road construction, power outages, and a street closure due to a fallen tree—that cause you to alter your planned route, but the change in plans doesn't change your destination.

As your approach Auntie Mim's, her house appears on the horizon; as you pull into her driveway, your extended family warmly greets you. You know you have arrived, even though you still don't know exactly what it looks like on the inside, what's cooking in her kitchen, or how her furniture is arranged. Nor do you know what exactly will happen in an hour from now.

Your life's purpose is like that. Your direction is always closely tied to your values. Opportunity will present itself, and you are ready to take advantage of all the opportunities that come your way or that you create, no matter what. There will be hiccups along the way, and the final destination will look somewhat different than what you initially imagined. But that destination will lead to the next opportunity, and on it goes.

The greatest problem many of us face is that we don't really know where we are going.

Paul Thompson, who co-teaches Confidence 101 course with me, presents this idea to our students this way. "How many of you have ever planned a vacation?" he asks.

About 95% of the people in the class raise their hands. "And how many of you have planned your life?" he then asks.

All the hands go down.

Anyone who has ever achieved a dream will tell you that she always had a grand vision, a master plan, of where she wanted to be in life. (She will also tell you that the realization of that dream always contained startling and unexpected components.) Some people arrive by way of having written goals, some arrive by way of sheer mental clarity, and some stumble upon their goal by chance.

The Value of Visualization

In *Finding Serenity in the Age of Anxiety*, Robert Gerzon gives us an interesting way of looking at worrying, planning, and visualization. He frames it thus:

1. To **worry** is anxiously to imagine a negative future, resulting in inaction or unproductive activity.

2. To **plan** is confidently to anticipate the future by taking practical steps to meet personal goals and turn potential problems into opportunities.

3. To **visualize** is to create a positive vision of the future—a best-case scenario.[30]

Notice the three stages? To worry is to stand still; to plan is to start moving; to visualize is to grow.

Consider Jane, who has just been "downsized."

She can **worry** about her situation. She can spin all the negative possibilities through her mind until she can't take it anymore. She can spin herself into sleepless nights and depression-laden days.

She can make a **plan** and take practical steps to line up interviews and options. She can pursue her dream job, or she can start that business she's always wanted to launch.

She can **visualize**, create in her mind's eye what her ultimate success will look like. She can document her dreams in her journal. She can create vision boards to remind herself continually of her vision, and she can commit to her vision by sharing it with trusted companions.

The power of visualization is what will take you there because ultimately you need to know WHAT you are pursuing. As Seth Godin says in his book *Tribes*, "The secret of leaderships is simple: Do what you believe in. Paint a picture of the future. Go there. People will follow."[31]

The Importance of Purpose

Have you ever envisioned yourself in the future? Perhaps you saw yourself at a university, or living in your first apartment, or working at a bookstore or professional office.

Tap into your past right now, and recall a vision that you had that came into being. Napoleon Hill, author of Think and Grow Rich, coined the term Definite Major Purpose.[32] Hill presented the Definite Major Purpose as a challenge to his readers, to make them ask themselves "What do I truly believe in?" According to Hill, 98% of people had no firm beliefs and thereby put true success firmly out of reach.

Hill's five-step formula for realizing your Definite Major Purpose:

1. Know that you can achieve your purpose. Promise yourself that you will persist until you succeed.

> *Many persons have a wrong idea of what constitutes true happiness. It is not attained through self-gratification but through fidelity to a worthy purpose.*
> — Helen Keller

2. Realize that what you think inside will be reflected on the outside. Get a clear mental image of yourself at the final destination, and revisit that image often.

3. Know that persistence produces results.

4. Record your purpose on paper (below).

5. Remember to leave everything in better shape than how you found it. That principle will serve you well. Integrity and honesty supersede negativity and greed.

If you follow these five simple steps, Hill proposes that others will believe in you because *you* will believe in yourself and your own purpose.

CALL TO ACTION

Napoleon Hill recommends that you put your Definite Major Purpose to paper. He also provides that formula in his book, which I am modifying here.

Write it out, and sign it, and then look at it twice a day to reinforce your message to you.

1. Become clear about what it is you wish to achieve. Be as clear and specific as you can. It is not sufficient to say "I want to be a writer." Instead say, "I will author a book on healthy living for children under five."

2. Determine what you will give, what you will do, or the services you will provide to achieve this objective. "I will provide invaluable nutritional information to parents, enabling them to give their children the best possible start in life. This information will lead to a reduction in child obesity and an increase in children's fitness levels." There is no such thing as getting something for nothing. Your object needs to be of value to others.

3. Set a date. I will do this by March 23rd, 201__.

4. Create a plan of action, and whether you are ready or not, begin implementing this plan. Do *something* today. Anything.

Write out a statement that clearly and concisely captures the previous four steps. Put it in your wallet. Duplicate it and post it all over your house. Read it at least twice a day, once in the morning and once at night. Make it the first and last thought of every day. And every time you read this statement, see yourself living the vision.

Chapter 3

GETTING TO KNOW YOUR INNER GENIUS

Education is, in brief, learning from experience—whether it's navigating interpersonal challenges at home, mastering a basketball or hockey puck, or producing music from a reed or rhythm from a tin can. If you are stretching yourself, you are learning.

As the mother of a five-year-old, I stand in awe of preschoolers. These young creatures learn at astounding rates.

- They completely master a language and seamlessly incorporate the rules of usage.
- They master physical feats, transforming from a state of non-voluntary movement to mastering balance, dexterity, and agility.
- They learn how to read people and respond in the most favorable way.
- They master the fine arts of marketing, salesmanship, influence, and negotiations.

And that's just in the first five years!

As they grow into teenagers, they will navigate the challenges presented by the educational system. Their creativity will fade as well-intentioned curriculums sharpen the development of their left-brain, logic, linear thinking, and rote mechanics. If they are lucky, they get right-brain exposure through a smattering of art classes, after-school music lessons, and physical education. After wrangling them through these educational systems, we then test their IQ.

Some people emphasize that formal schooling is the most formative component in your life, but I disagree. As mentioned earlier, you are more likely to remember a particular teacher (good or bad) than a grade. Even though we spend many hours in the school setting, most learning is done on the edges of our lives.

In your first two decades of life, you may have experienced any number of difficult learning lessons: your peers tossed you through the turbulence of cliques and leveraged friendships. The tsunami of pubescence broke your spirit. Your first "true love" broke your heart. Then, in adulthood, a sea of media and advertisements envelops you each day, telling you how a "normal" woman should look, live, and love.

It's your job to wade through all this muck and mire and figure out who you are and where (and how) you stand. Dealing with grades in a mostly subjective educational system is part of identity formation, but in many cases not the primary one, and almost never the only one.

If you really liked your formal education, or if you were determined to prolong your entry into the so-called real world, you may have pursued "higher education."[19] When you enter a college or university, you realize you and only you are responsible for attending class. Notes from your mom are no longer required. You navigate your way through your new social life, and you have to find your own clubs and social circles. It becomes your job to figure out each professor's grading system in order to get a good grade.

What benefit will the good grades bring? In spite of the emphasis placed on them, in the professional world, *they don't matter.* The only institutes that care about your grades are those that assign them. A copy of your transcript will rarely (*if ever*) be required for most jobs, entrepreneurial ventures, start-up loans, dates, marriages, fishing licenses, or any other aspect in life *outside* of the ivory tower of academia.[20]

Should you believe yourself to be ready to think for yourself, you can enter into a master's degree program. This time is the only one in your formal education when you are entitled to an opinion. If you continue on to a doctoral program, you learn that you have *no* opinion, and every statement you make must be accompanied by a reference to an entire body of work.

When you're done with academia, you're tossed back into the ring of life to see how quickly you can apply what you know and succeed at whatever life throws your way.[21]

However, when you are completely removed from the academic circus—I mean circuit—you are free to focus more intently on your true education, uncover your authentic talents, and explore your true genius.

UNCOVERING YOUR AUTHENTIC TALENTS

Charles Dickens excelled linguistically. Many of his early publications were submitted as first and yet final drafts. What flowed from his pen was integrally connected to his inner strength and talents. Likewise, Albert Einstein could actually SEE himself traveling on a beam of light[22]—an abstract ability indeed—and he was a mathematical genius. Vincent Van Gogh lived to paint. He tried his hand at traditional moneymaking (working as a Methodists minister's assistant, a pastor, and eventually as a missionary), but his brother Theo convinced him to pursue painting.

It's easy to identify talents once the story has been complete, and history has been given the space to remember generously the good times. We often forget the hurdles it took to get there. Dickens' formal education was interrupted at an early age; when he was twelve, Charles Dickens was working ten-hour days at a warehouse and earning additional money on the side shining shoes. Einstein was considered a daydreamer at school and was considered an academic failure. And were it not for the financial generosity of his brother, Vincent Van Gogh would probably not have quit his day job. In fact, Vincent Van Gogh died poor and unappreciated. His paintings were locally purchased and hung on the front doors of houses to ward off evil spirits, but other than that, they were deemed to be valueless.

Henry Winkler, who played "The Fonz" in the 1970s sitcom *Happy Days*, was not diagnosed until he was thirty-one with the "learning challenge" of dyslexia. He had gone through his school years being called "dumb dog" by his parents and wore his self-esteem around his ankles for many years.[23] Today, Winkler writes children's books designed to celebrate the absolute brilliance and talent he believes (as do I) that all children possess, regardless of how they are ranked by the educational system.

In 2009, Winkler spoke at Winston School, a private school that serves students with dyslexia and other learning disabilities. "It doesn't matter if you don't get a subject," he told the audience. "How you learn has nothing to do with how great you are. Your job is to find out what your gift is, what your contribution will be."[24]

In the book *Think and Grow Rich*, Napoleon Hill explores this same topic:

Somewhere in your make-up lies sleeping the seed of achievement, which, if aroused and put into action, would carry you to heights such as you may never have hoped to attain.

Just as a master musician may cause the most beautiful strains of music to pour forth from the strings of a violin, so may you arouse the genius which lies asleep in your brain, and cause it to drive you upward to whatever goal you may wish to achieve.[25]

What really matters is this: It's not *how smart you are* that matters—it's *how you are smart*. If you can tap into what truly motivates you—where when you are engaged you lose yourself to timelessness—that is where your talent lies.

No academic system will ever work exclusively to unveil your inner genius. Perhaps this is the first time you've ever heard anyone express such a notion, but when properly armed with the right information, I am confident you will rise to the occasion!

How You Are Smart

Our current academic system focuses primarily on one type of intelligence: the logical/mathematical type.[26]

I grew up doing intelligence quotient (IQ) questionnaires in school, where you had one questionnaire booklet and an answer sheet, and you had to select an answer from A to E for each question in the booklet. Then you were given a pencil and told to color in the circles. (And God forbid you should draw outside the circle, confuse the marking machine, and skew your results!) About 500 questions asked to find the next logical image in a sequence or figure out which one was not like the others.

> *When sleeping women wake, mountains move.*
> — **Chinese Proverb**

Sometimes, if I were not done in the last five minutes, I would randomly color in the circles based on the patterns I saw emerging on my answer sheet. At other times, I would select the next five D answers, the next five C answers, or whatever pattern struck me as fun.

Although we were subjected to these tests for about five years, we never got our results. To this day I don't know what happened to them. Perhaps the principal kept the results. Perhaps our parents were told. Perhaps the school psychologist was forewarned.

Recently, however, new types of "awarenesses" have emerged. It is now thought that dyslexics actually function on a three-dimensional plane, whereas "non-dyslexics" function on a two-dimensional plane. For instance, writing occurs in two dimensions. The written English language begins at the top left corner and the words are written in a straight line, left to right; then the writing jumps back to the left side and progresses to the right. Dyslexics frequently jumble letters and numbers because this kind of two-dimensional sequencing is not dominant in their perceptions. Get them to envision a three-dimensional construct, and they excel beyond expectations. Dyslexics may excel as architects and spatial visionaries (there is some suspicion that Einstein himself was dyslexic).

In other words, what was once considered a learning disability is now being reconsidered as a non-standardized type of talent.

GARDNER'S MULTIPLE INTELLIGENCES

In 1983, Howard Gardner proposed that there are multiple forms of intelligence, expanding far beyond the traditional understanding of IQ. Many now subscribe to the belief that every human being under normal circumstances has a talent in at least one and sometimes several areas.

By answering the questions in the following section, you can gauge which forms of intelligence (talents, areas of genius, and your personal areas of strength) are your strongest, and which are your weakest. This process will enable you to make the most of your existing abilities. You will also see where, by acknowledging your weaknesses, you can consider working in collaboration with others.

A questionnaire follows on the next few pages. As you progress through the questions, keep the following caveats in mind.

1. Many different types of intelligence and personality type tests exist.

2. Each differing type adds some level of value and deepens your understanding of yourself.

3. Any result indicates a *preference*. A good example is handedness. You may be predominantly left-handed or predominantly right-handed, yet you can use both hands.

4. Your brain is the most powerful machine known to humankind, and you are capable of learning any new skill. Were you left-handed and lost your left hand, you would adapt and start living with the use of your right hand.

5. There is NO SUCH THING AS STUPID. Calling someone stupid simply means we don't share that person's way of understanding something.

EXPOSING YOUR TALENTS: A QUESTIONNAIRE

Check the box ☑ if the sentence applies to you and then add the number of boxes you have checked in the last line.

VERBAL-LINGUISTIC

☐ You enjoy word play, puns, and tongue twisters.

☐ You read everything.

☐ You're a good storyteller or writer.

☐ You like referencing things you've read or heard.

☐ You like to do crossword puzzles and play Scrabble.

☐ You use complex words.

☐ In school, you preferred English, history, and social studies.

☐ You often engage in verbal repartee and debates.

☐ You talk through problems and ask questions.

☐ You can readily absorb information from the radio.

Total number of checks (☑): _____

VISUAL-SPATIAL

☐ You love visiting art galleries.

☐ You like to record events with photographs or video.

☐ You find yourself doodling when talking or thinking.

☐ You like using maps to navigate.

☐ You enjoy visual games such as puzzles and mazes.

☐ You can take things apart and put them together.

☐ In school, art classes engaged and excited you.

☐ You often draw diagrams to make your point.

☐ You can see things from a different perspective.

☐ You prefer books that are heavily illustrated.

Total number of checks (☑): _____

MUSICAL-AUDITORY

☐ You can play a musical instrument.

☐ You sing on key.

☐ You easily remember melodies.

☐ You often listen to music at home and in your car.

☐ You find yourself tapping in time to music.

☐ You can identify different musical instruments.

☐ Commercial jingles often pop into your head.

☐ You can't imagine life without music.

☐ You often whistle or hum a tune.

☐ You like to play music while you're working.

Total number of checks (☑): _____

BODY-KINESTHETIC

☐ You like sports and physical exercise.

☐ You buy items that require assembly.

☐ You figure out problems when exercising.

☐ You don't mind getting up on the dance floor.

☐ You like the most adrenaline-inducing rides at the fair.

☐ You physically handle something in order to understand it.

☐ You loved physical education in school.

☐ You talk with your hands.

☐ You like rough-and-tumble play with children.

☐ You learn more by doing than looking at a manual.

Total number of checks (☑): _____

LOGICAL-MATHEMATICAL

☐ You enjoy working with numbers.

☐ You're interested in new scientific advances.

☐ You can easily balance your checkbook.

☐ You like detailed itineraries for vacation trips.

☐ You like brain-teasers and other logic puzzles.

☐ You find logical flaws in things people say and do.

☐ Math and science were your favorite subjects.

☐ You like to have examples to support a point of view.

☐ You systematically solve problems.

☐ You like to organize things into appropriate categories.

Total number of checks (☑): _____

NATURALIST

☐ You keep or like pets.

☐ You can name different types of plants.

☐ You know much about how the body works.

☐ You are conscious of tracks, nests, and wildlife.

☐ You like to farm or fish.

☐ You are a keen gardener.

☐ You understand global environmental issues.

☐ You like astronomy and/or evolution theories.

☐ You like to learn about social issues, psychology, and motivation.

☐ You are concerned about conservation and sustainability.

Total number of checks (☑): _____

INTERPERSONAL	**INTRAPERSONAL**
☐ You like working with other people.	☐ You keep a personal diary.
☐ You take pride in being a mentor.	☐ You like your "quiet time."
☐ People tend to come to you for advice.	☐ You set your own goals.
	☐ You are an independent thinker.
☐ You prefer team sports to individual sports.	☐ You have solitary hobbies and interests.
☐ You like games that involve other people.	☐ You like your own company.
☐ You're a social butterfly.	☐ You'd spend your vacation in an isolated hilltop cabin.
☐ You have several very close personal friends.	☐ You know your own strengths and weaknesses.
☐ You communicate well and can resolve disputes.	☐ You have attended self-improvement workshops.
☐ You take the lead with no hesitation.	☐ You would like to work for yourself.
☐ You talk over problems with others.	

Total number of checks (☑): _____   Total number of checks (☑): _____

Transfer your scores here:

Verbal-Linguistic	_____	Visual-Spatial	_____
Musical-Auditory	_____	Body-Kinesthetic	_____
Logical-Mathematical	_____	Naturalist	_____
Interpersonal	_____	Intrapersonal	_____

QUIZ RESULTS PER SECTION

0: This area is definitely not one where you have a natural talent. This is neither good nor bad; it simply is what it is. Consider it like having a preferred hand for writing or eating with a fork. This score means this hand is not the preferred one.

1-4: You have a slight inclination toward this talent but it is not dominant. If you wanted to, you could hone this strength. Bear in mind that successful entrepreneurs and business people focus almost exclusively on their strengths and delegate the rest.

5-7: You are somewhat talented in this area. If you applied yourself to sharpening this talent, you could truly flourish. Perhaps you haven't had the time in your life to focus on what you consider to be your hobby; perhaps you have always been discouraged in this area because of other peoples' beliefs.

8-10: This is your innate talent, and it comes to you easily. You do it naturally and without thinking.

Now compare the areas in which you scored the highest with the lists below to learn more about your natural talents or affinities.

Verbal-Linguistic

Verbal-linguistically talented people work with spoken or written words. They display great facility with words and languages, and they are keenly sensitive to the meaning and sequencing of words.

- ✓ They are good at reading, writing, and telling stories.
- ✓ They can easily memorize lyrics, passages, and dates.
- ✓ They tend to learn by using three faculties: seeing (reading), feeling (taking notes), and hearing (listening to lectures, discussion, and debate).
- ✓ They excel at explaining, teaching, oration, or persuasive speaking.
- ✓ They learn foreign languages very easily.
- ✓ They have high verbal memory and recall.
- ✓ They can easily understand and manipulate syntax and word structure.

This type of intelligence is found in comedians, copywriters, editors, English teachers, journalists, lawyers, linguists, media consultants, orators, philosophers, poets, politicians, PR consultants, speakers, teachers, trainers, translators, TV and radio presenters, voice-over artists, and writers. Famous examples include Charles Dickens, Abraham Lincoln, T. S. Eliot, and Winston Churchill.

Visual-Spatial

Visual-spatially talented people work primarily with vision and spatial judgment. People with strong visual-spatial intelligence are capable of thinking in pictures and can "see" both the abstract and the literal. They are very good at "seeing" themselves in a particular scenario.

- ✓ They are very good at visualizing.
- ✓ They can mentally manipulate objects.
- ✓ They are often proficient at solving puzzles.
- ✓ They have a strong visual memory.
- ✓ They are often artistically inclined.
- ✓ They have a very good sense of direction.
- ✓ They have very good hand-eye coordination, a characteristic shared with the bodily-kinesthetic intelligence.

Careers that suit those with this type of intelligence include architects, artists, beauty consultants, cartoonists, cosmeticians, designers, engineers, inventors, photographers, sailors, sculptors, story-boarders, strategic planners, town-planners, and visionaries. Famous examples include Picasso, Frank Lloyd Wright, and Albert Einstein.

Musical-Auditory

Musical intelligence has to do with rhythm, music, and hearing. Those who have a high level of musical-rhythmic intelligence can create, understand, and appreciate music to a much higher degree. They thrive on the complexities of a wide variety of musical genres.

- ✓ They display great sensitivity to sounds, rhythms, tones, and music.
- ✓ They have good (or even absolute) pitch.
- ✓ They are able to sing well.
- ✓ They play several musical instruments.
- ✓ They compose music.
- ✓ They learn best via lecture.
- ✓ They often use songs or rhythms to learn and memorize information.
- ✓ They may work best with music playing in the background.

Careers that suit those with this type of intelligence include acoustic engineers, composers, conductors, disc-jockeys, entertainers, environment and noise advisors, instrumentalists, music producers, musicians, orators, party planners, piano tuners, recording engineers, singers, voice coaches, and writers (to a certain extent). Famous examples include Mozart, Leonard Bernstein, and Ray Charles.

Body-Kinesthetic

People who are body-kinesthetic oriented focus primarily on bodily movement. They can use their body as a tool in either self-expression (as in dance) or toward achieving athletic goals.

- ✓ They learn best by moving around rather than reading or hearing about a subject.
- ✓ They are good at physical activities that apply muscle memory (sports or dance).
- ✓ They may enjoy acting or performing.
- ✓ They are good at building and making things.
- ✓ They use words or images to remember things.

Careers that suit those with this type of intelligence include actors, acupuncturists, adventurers, athletes, builders, chefs, craftspeople, dancers, demonstrators, divers, doctors, drivers, ergonomists, firefighters, fishermen, gardeners, healers, osteopaths, performance artists, physical training instructors, soldiers, and surgeons. Famous examples include Charlie Chaplin, Ginger Rogers, Fred Astaire, and Michael Jordan. The kinesthetic style is also referred to as Physical, Tactile, or "Touchy Feely."

Logical-Mathematical

This area or talent correlates most strongly with traditional concepts of intelligence or IQ. Those with strength in the logical-mathematical area thrive on logic, abstractions, reasoning, and numbers.

✓ They use their strong numeric comprehension for activities such as mathematics, chess, and computer programming.

✓ They like to use their reasoning capabilities.

✓ They are good at abstract patterns of recognition.

✓ They employ scientific thinking.

✓ They like investigation.

✓ They can perform complex calculations.

Careers that suit those with this type of intelligence include accountants, analysts, bankers, bookmakers, computer experts, detectives, directors, doctors, economists, engineers, insurance brokers, lawyers, mathematicians, negotiators, researchers, scientists, statisticians, traders, and troubleshooters. One famous example is John Dewey, the founder of the Dewey Decimal System.

Naturalist

Naturalists enjoy anything that has to do with nature, nurturing, and relating information to one's natural surroundings.

✓ They are highly sensitive to the natural world.

✓ They see the human species as *one of many* that live and thrive on the planet.

- ✓ They nurture and grow things.
- ✓ They care for, tame, and interact with animals with ease.
- ✓ They can discern changes in weather or similar fluctuations in their natural surroundings.
- ✓ They enjoy recognizing and classifying things.
- ✓ They connect current experience with prior knowledge.
- ✓ They learn best when the subject involves collecting and analyzing.
- ✓ They don't enjoy learning subjects with little or no connection to nature.
- ✓ They learn more through being outside or using their body.

Careers that suit those with this type of intelligence include biologists, conservationists, farmers, gardeners, naturalists, and scientists. Famous examples include Charles Darwin, E. O. Wilson, David Suzuki, and Jacques Cousteau.

Interpersonal

Those with interpersonal talents excel in interaction with others. They empathize with other individuals, and they can easily sense the moods, desires, and motivations of other people.

- ✓ They tend to be extroverts who are sensitive to others' moods, feelings, temperaments, and motivations.
- ✓ They work cooperatively as part of a group.
- ✓ They communicate effectively.
- ✓ They empathize easily with others.
- ✓ They are natural and effective leaders.
- ✓ They learn best by working with others.
- ✓ They enjoy discussion and debate.

Careers that suit those with this type of intelligence include advertising professionals, clergy, coaches, counselors, doctors, educators, healers, human resources professionals, leaders, managers, mediators, mentors, organizers, politicians, psychologists, salespeople, social workers, teachers, and

> *Share your strengths, not your weaknesses.*
> — attributed to Yogi Bhajan

therapists. Famous examples include Gandhi, Ronald Reagan, Mother Teresa, and Oprah Winfrey. This type of intelligence is associated with the Intrapersonal intelligence outlined below and what is termed Emotional Intelligence (EQ).

Intrapersonal

People with strong intrapersonal talents are introspective and self-reflective, and they have a keen understanding of their own moods, motivations, and desires.

- ✓ They are typically introverts and prefer to work alone.
- ✓ They have a high degree of self-awareness.
- ✓ They understand their own emotions, goals, and motivations.
- ✓ They have an affinity for thought-based pursuits such as philosophy.
- ✓ They learn best when allowed to concentrate on the subject by themselves.
- ✓ They often have a high level of perfectionism.

Careers that suit those with this type of intelligence include counselors, philosophers, psychologists, scientists, theologians, and writers. Famous examples include Sigmund Freud, Eleanor Roosevelt, and Plato.

BENEFITS TO KNOWING YOUR TALENT

When you understand where your areas of genius and talent lie, you can start seeing yourself in a different way and can expand your avenues of action.

Perhaps you want to be a movie director, but you are no James Cameron (director of *Avatar*, *Titanic*, *Aliens,* and *Rambo* to name but a few). Perhaps you are a great visionary or a great people person. Perhaps you have a knack for sound effects and audio inclusions. By knowing where your strengths lie, you can use that knowledge to shape your life's mission.

Find the Right Business Opportunities

In the past, I have joined several network marketing companies, including travel agencies, health food industries, education communities, and communications organizations. In each case, I convinced myself that the incentive message was true: "Here is a proven product with proven success stories, and if you follow this proven model, you too can succeed."

Each case had its proven product with success stories and a proven model of success. However, I was not the *right person* with the *right talent* that best suited that particular model of success. I was certified as a travel agent, but I am not a big traveler. I was selling dietary products without any knowledge, experience, or interest in nutrition. While I knew that each product had a very lucrative market, I didn't realize I was not the right person to offer it to that market.

Before signing up with any company (or any entrepreneurial or professional venture), be sure your talents are a good fit for the company and its offerings.

Build a Better Team

When an athlete wants to improve her game, she may be advised to analyze and strengthen her weaknesses until they disappear.

In the business world, it is important to recognize your weaknesses (and compensate for them by leveraging the rest of the team built around the business), but it is even more important to recognize your talents, and it is absolutely critical to focus your efforts on your talents.

While many others may share your talent, when you give it your unique spin and insights, you will turn your talents into a successful business venture.

If you are a great visionary but lack follow-through, work with someone who is very detail-oriented. If you are musically talented but cannot be bothered with the accounting end of your business, you MUST find people who support your dream and can handle the finances for you.

Make Better Decisions

When you are deciding to take a course, signing up to follow a particular mentor, or weighing an important decision, previously agonizing decisions can become easy if you know your particular talent.

Stephanie Frank, author of *The Accidental Millionaire*, describes a valuable exercise where you list the top values in your life, the things for which you stand. You pare the list down to five and then cross out two more so you are left with three.[27] According to Frank, these three represent your life's purpose. When confronted with any decision, you simply need to ask yourself what will lead you closer to that purpose.

Knowing your primary talents and where your inner genius lies will help you to identify your top three values.

For example, my top three values are service, joy, and spirituality. Whenever I have a decision to make, I ask myself which option allows me to be of greater service, which will result in greater joy for my family and myself, and which option aligns with my spiritual beliefs.

When an option fulfils all three criteria, the decision is easy.

Aligning Talents with Your Causes

Humans have two primary motivations: to move *toward pleasure*, or to move *away from pain*. We spend most of our lives moving away. So let's start thinking about what it is that moves us toward pleasure. What propels you out of bed in the morning, eager to embrace the day? What positive incentives spur you into action?

If you don't know, consider the causes in which you believe. Your causes are what you are inclined to move toward, actions you are inclined to take because you *want* to do them, not because you *have to*. Your causes tend to employ your natural talents. If you've separated them, however, you have "what you do for money" on the one hand and "what you do for fun" on the other.

One of my lifelong causes has been the pursuit of justice. In 1975 when I was in the fifth grade, my family moved to a new neighborhood, a small town with a population of about two thousand. If you didn't have a great-grandfather buried in one of the local cemeteries, you were considered an outsider. In addition, we were German and my father deigned to build a house from scratch. And as if that weren't enough, I had short, curly hair in a time when Farrah Fawcett–style feathered hair was hot. Needless to say, I was a prime target for taunting and teasing at school.

Then a new girl came to the school, Jennifer. The girls who used to torment me relentlessly now gathered to pick on this even newer girl. Fresh fodder!

At first, I was tremendously relieved that they had finally something to do other than pick on me. Jennifer had a last name that was unfortunately close to "Weebles." Weebles, if you are too young or old to remember, was a trademark for a set of roly-poly egg-shaped toys; besides her last name, Jennifer had the compounded misfortune of also being somewhat plump. The girls at school, always hungry for a new common (female) enemy, found their way to her in a flash.

One girl was the ringleader, the instigator of all the schoolyard teasing. She was the bane of my existence, and now she was determined to inflict the same destruction on Jennifer. On this fateful day, this ringleader gathered the recess girls around Jennifer and started the chant, "Weebles wobble but they don't fall down." Persistence prevails. Even in the negative. And it didn't take long for Jennifer to break down and cry.

To this day, I still have no idea what possessed me, but I broke into that circle and marched up to that bossy little ringleader. Without any hesitation, I took her by the collar of her coat and *slammed* her up against the schoolyard wall and informed her that she was never EVER to tease Jennifer again.

The ringleader slumped to the ground and slunk away. She didn't look at me as she left, but apparently that warning registered deep within her. The teasing aimed at Jennifer stopped, although the girls continued to tease me.

This teasing, this injustice, has throughout my life inspired me to reach beyond my comfort zone without even thinking about it and to stand up for someone or something important to me. The cause of justice is greater than my fears and far supersedes them. It gives me strength, and it propels me forward.

YOUR UNIQUE TALENTS

My five-year-old daughter is just beginning her entry into the academic world where her intelligence will be subjectively measured by one person (the teacher) and measured relative to her peers. She may be ranked as one of the top 10% in her class, or she may be ranked as one of the 10% that makes the upper 90% possible.

When I look at my daughter and her peers, I see a wide range of brilliance and beauty, all reflected differently in each of them. One is a more spirited, adventurous, tree-climber; another gets buried deep in the fantasy land of her imagination; yet another is brilliant at social interaction and has climbed to the top of the social hierarchy. However, these same children will be measured through the single lens of academic grading.

You have absolutely perfected what it takes to be you. The teachers in your life may have said that you need to be logical and charismatic to succeed, when in fact your true nature is intuition and self-awareness. No time is better than the present to discard other people's beliefs and celebrate your natural and genius self, talents and all!

CALL TO ACTION

Each of us has a talent, an area in which we primarily excel.

1. Go back and review the previous questionnaire that assessed your multiple intelligences. Perhaps you identify with one of Gardner's areas of talent, or perhaps you scored high in three or four.

2. Review your answers to the questionnaire and record the four talents in which you excel, in order from highest score to lowest.

3. Now think back on your life using the following questions as a guideline.

    a. As a child (ages 1-10), what were your top two favorite activities?

    b. As a child, in what kind of activity did you have a sense of timelessness?

    c. As a pre-teen and teen (ages 10-20), to which clique did most of your school peers belong? Your peers at home? Your peers during the summer?

    d. As a pre-teen and teen, what was the most delightful trouble you ever got in?

    e. What illicit activities, if any, did you engage in? How long did those activities last? What did you gain from those activities? What did you lose?

    f. As a young adult (ages 20-30), what were your most significant growth quests? World travel? Your first job? A business? A family? What single event most impacted your development?

    g. As a maturing adult (ages 30-50), which sideline activities did you incorporate into your life? What did you do to escape and replenish?

h. As a mature adult (age 50+), where do you get a sense of timelessness?

4. Now go back to the top of this list and correlate your top four talents with these experiences.

This process will help you recall some forgotten passions and point you to your true talents.

Next, you need to align your talents to your values. What are your strongest values? What means the most to you? The chart below lists a number of values, and you are free to add your own.

VALUE	High	Medium	Low	VALUE	High	Medium	Low
Acceptance				Money			
Ambition				Popularity			
Competition				Power			
Contribution				Predictability			
Cooperation				Privacy			
Excitement				Recognition			
Fairness				Respect			
Family				Security			
Freedom				Sense of humor			
Friendship				Service			
Happiness				Status			
Helpfulness				Success			
Honesty				Team work			
Independence				Trust			
Leadership				Wealth			
Leisure Time				Wisdom			
Love				Work			
Loyalty							

Rank each value from your list from the least important to the most. In other words, if you have seventeen values, begin your list by identifying the *least* important in relation to the others by first looking at all the values you rated low, then medium, then high. If you get stuck, remember to rank the values only in relation to the others that remain.

Once you have identified your top five values, you then need to articulate specifically what that value means to you. Different people will have different definitions for the same value. For instance, if you rank "Family" as high, think about what family means to you. It may mean living in the same town as your immediate family. It may mean weekly connecting with your siblings who are scattered worldwide. It may mean providing shelter from the storms of life for your new family. Be sure to create your own unique definition.

Top 5 Values	Extended Definition

In completing this exercise, you have identified some of your talents and values. When you can incorporate those talents and values into a singular activity, you will have identified a core passion. Core passions act as your life's compass.

Section II

COLLABORATION

A Hunting Party

A
Hunting party
Sometimes has a greater chance
Of flushing love and God
Out into the open
Than a warrior
All
Alone

— **Hafiz,** *The Gift* (P. 26)

Collaboration is the second strategy of the unstoppable woman. As we work with others, our world, our strengths and our opportunities expand.

It is true that on one level, we exist alone. Your personal perspective—the world as you see, hear, and experience it—is unique. The amalgamation of your past experiences, interpretations, and emotional connections provides a focal point that no one but you can experience.

At the same time, you co-exist with others. How you think and feel, what you choose to aspire to, and how you design your life is heavily influenced by the existence of the people around you. In its positive form, this influence is known as collaboration.

If you have ever learned a new skill, you have already participated collaboratively. When you learned to walk, your guardian helped you physically by holding your hand and protecting you when you fell as well as by modeling the act of walking for you.

When you learned to read, to write, to do math, or to recite Shakespeare, you did so with the assistance of a teacher, a parent or guardian, and perhaps classmates and friends.

When you learned to drive a car, you watched from the backseat or you took lessons from a driving school.

You've already participated in the collaborative model. This section will help you to infuse your collaborative skills with increased intentionality so you can access them at will.

Chapter 5

UNDERSTANDING THE POWER OF COLLABORATION

COLLABORATION VERSUS COOPERATION

There's the pragmatic climbing-of-the-ladder through cooperation, and there's the exponential forward propulsion of collaboration. Those who know how to tap into the power of collaboration benefit from the knowledge and expertise of those before them and those around them, so they move forward at an accelerated rate. As Sir Isaac Newton said, "If I have seen further, it is only by standing on the shoulders of giants."

Giants come in all shapes, sizes, genders, and colors. They are the great names imbedded in the canons of history, and they also walk among us. While names like Henry Ford and Albert Einstein readily come to mind, we can also draw from the likes of Sappho, Joan of Arc, Florence Nightingale, Rosa Parks, Mary Baker Eddy, and Eleanor Roosevelt. There are the people who shape your country, your region, and your town. There are those who influence your neighborhood and your children's education.

A giant is one who has previously forged the path of travel. She is the person who has already arrived at your destination and is inviting you to walk in her footsteps.

No Man Is an Island
*No man is an island
entire of itself; every man
is a piece of the continent,
a part of the main; if a
clod be washed away by
the sea, Europe is the less,
as well as if a promontory
were, as well as any
manner of thy friends or
of thine own were; any
man's death diminishes
me, because I am involved
in mankind. And therefore
never send to know for
whom the bell tolls; it tolls
for thee.*
— John Donne,
*MEDITATION XVII
Devotions upon Emergent
Occasions*

Do you want to start your own storefront? Well, there have been many who have already done so and would let you learn from their achievements as well as their mistakes. Want to start a network marketing business? Many people with incredible success stories are eager to share their knowledge with you. Want to start an online business? Many others have already successfully navigated your current aspiration, and they will happily collaborate with you to help you avoid the pitfalls they encountered on their own journeys.

Collaboration is much more than simply "getting along with other people." It goes far beyond the old model of cooperation or compromise where "you meet me in the middle" and both parties win a little and lose a little. True collaboration is about expanding possibilities. It's about building a productive team, creating a dynamic collective that goes far beyond what an individual could do alone, and creating a universal "win-win-win." You win. Your partners win. The recipients of your service or product win.

All successful collaborations are twofold: they build alliances, and these alliances benefit all players. To collaborate successfully, one must acknowledge that working in association with others has greater potential than working alone. In order for collaboration to work at its fullest level, you must have high levels of both cooperation and assertiveness.

High Cooperation

1. Shared Objective. There must be both the belief and the shared dedicated drive to move toward the same final outcome. Cooperation is high.

2. Interpersonal Bonds. The bonds that develop in a shared pursuit are strong and unifying, and each player is committed to sharing her strengths.

3. Generous Outlook. Helping others is essential. You succeed when you help others in their success.

High Assertiveness

1. Complex Interpersonal Engagement. Collaboration is not perpetual Happy Land. Relationships are complex and multifaceted, and they must be allowed to exist as such.

2. Safe. A sense of belonging must be nurtured. It is okay to say what's on your mind. In fact, it's critical for you to do so. It is okay to make mistakes. It is okay to voice dissent.

These components work together to create high levels of assertiveness and cooperation.

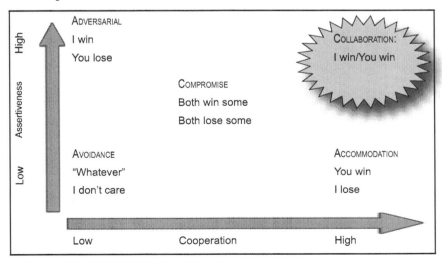

The keys to successful collaboration:

1. Get to know the people who have already accomplished what you intend to achieve.

2. Consciously set out to work with them and tap their knowledge to boost your own success.

3. Complement your weaknesses with the strengths of others.

Whether you're starting a new venture, growing an old one, or pursuing a life's passion, you should always be asking yourself the following two questions. What in your immediate surroundings did an innovative giant create? How could you use that giant's ideas to further your own life as a parent, employee, artist, or entrepreneur?

CALL TO ACTION

Take an inventory of the people in your life you consider to be successful.

1. Whom do you know who has been driven to succeed at her dreams, no matter what?

2. How did she do it? How does she do it? Interview the person if you can to find out what enables her to have such a clear vision and follow it to the end.

3. How can you follow the same path? What aspects of this person's success can you incorporate into your life? Vision boards, goal setting, mission statements?

How do Women Collaborate?

To be frank, not very well.

There's a myth that is currently circulating in our gentle society. This myth says that women are natural collaborators, peacemakers, and nurturers; that in times of crisis, women gather in solidarity to "tend and befriend."[33] Fight and flight, the myth contends, is a male strategy; we women know better.

We have this fantastic mythical view of ourselves that we are nurturers above all else, and that if only women ran the world, what a lovely place it would be.

Yet, at the same time, each and every one of us is familiar with the boss from hell. She's also known as the "Queen Bee Boss," nicely encapsulated by the character of Miranda Priestly, editor in chief of *Runway Magazine* in the 2006 movie *The Devil Wears Prada*.

A 2008 study from the University of Toronto showed that a woman who works for another woman suffers a higher degree of stress than if either she worked for a man, or if a man worked for that same woman.[34] Another article from the same paper says that there's a (nonsensical) "sisterhood" belief that says it is the men who makes us so incredibly devious. To put it bluntly, that is a load of bull. "Actually, it isn't men—it's girls; it's the girls they used to know and the girls they used to be, and anybody who ever went to an all-girls school will know exactly what I mean. There is no thuggery among boys that matches the viciousness that a gang of girls can inflict upon the victim of their choice."[35]

For the most part, women are especially challenged when it comes to collaboration. Our relationships with other women are intense. We have intense connections with each other: our best friends are best friends

> *Great minds discuss ideas, average minds discuss events, small minds discuss people.*
> — Eleanor Roosevelt

forever, and the same applies to our enemies. We passionately cling to our intense connections. And we don't have to scratch too far below the surface to find constant animosity, competition, and downright cattiness.

I grew up in a small town where sports were the mechanism that brought neighboring towns together. In a farming community where your closest neighbor was a thirty-minute walk away, sports provided social engagement. Back in the day, the boys placed hockey and the girls played broomball. The gender differences were glaringly obvious. The boys played hard and mean, but when the game was over, the fights that happened on the ice were left on the ice. Afterwards, the boys would all play nicely back at school. The girls, on the other hand, played for life. Fights that happened on the ice were solemnly wrapped up in memory and relived for months after each event. Loyalties were sworn, and enemy camps were born. What happened on the ice lived on in the classroom, at community dances, and in the perpetual gossip that venomously wiped about in quick whispers and backhanded comments.

While I can't claim that this experience is universal (I haven't done the statistical legwork), I know many women have experienced it in their lifetimes. My sister-in-law sees the same thing happening today in her soccer team, half a world away, three long decades later. Every woman I speak with understands the Queen Bee boss-from-hell. Every woman has either lived through or otherwise witnessed the devastating power of the female high school clique, brought to heightened media attention with the brutal murder of Reena Virk in 1997.[36]

Woman's Inhumanity to Woman, by Phyllis Chesler, tells us what many of us already know: girls are raised in a context of adversity and high competition with other girls.[37] This pressure begins our default female/female interactions in adulthood. The girls who band together in the playgrounds, schoolyards, and shopping malls are not renowned for their willingness to welcome other girls into their circles; rather, they are tightly knit cliques with specific hierarchies and rules of conduct. Violating these rules can result in psychological punishment (exclusion, gossip, being rendered invisible or worse, being rendered visible) or even physical punishment ranging from minor physical assaults to beatings to death.

You may have heard a woman say she has always gotten along better with men than with women. She might go on to tell you that women can be more competitive, gossipy, unapproachable, and "clique-ish" than men.

You may also have heard a woman say that the worst boss she ever worked for was another woman. This female boss-from-hell might be described as "absolutely unsupportive, closed, distant, and aloof."

In both instances, these women are stuck in the playground/shopping mall mentality, and the reasons are deeply seeded in psychological survival.

Many times, girls are raised to wage psychological warfare with other girls. They learn to leverage exclusion and employ gossip to damage another girl's social status. When Sonya sees the words "Sonya is a slut" written in a girl's bathroom stall, her war has started. Boys, on the other hand, resolve a conflict by fighting it out, physically or otherwise. In most cases, when the fight is over, the conflict is forgotten. Boys confront and move on—girls drag a grudge out for years.

Remember the story I told you about the bullying of Jennifer and myself earlier? It was spearheaded by girls. The boys were busy releasing their energy through their physical games at recess and lunch hour. In my earlier elementary years, tyrannical girls were led by Glenda and Adele; these two would lead the charge with anywhere from two to seven other girls, and walk through the schoolyard chanting damaging mantras about other girls in the school. Before them it was Tammy and Kirsten. In later years, Karen and Cindy stepped up to the plate. This pairing is all too familiar to anyone who has roamed a school's hallways. There is always the primary tyrant, the she-wolf, whose hostility is adoringly sustained by a primary disciple, the eager dog who is all-too-willing to please.

Whether it is a difference of estrogen or testosterone, or whether it is nature versus nurture, the question is academic. What matters more is that women have an amazing opportunity to walk away from this damaging mindset and instead to embrace each other as collaborators. Do we wage psychological warfare against other women, or are we going to work with that incredibly powerful entity known as "woman" to nurture exponential growth, productivity, and change for the better? My hope is for the latter.

Many women change careers about halfway through life. I attribute midlife changes in part to an evolving identity that has grown deeper than our skin to celebrate our inner qualities. I attribute it to the demise of the playground/mall mentality of female-to-female relationships as we discover the incredible power of strongly bonded, authentic, constructive, transformative female-to-female relationships.

SELECTING COLLABORATORS

Once you know your strengths and have clarity on where you are going, you need to align yourself with the people who are going to be the best and most effective teachers for *you*. Who is helping you to move your dream forward can define the degree of your success.

Let me tell you about Rebecca, whose aspiration was to learn how to ride a motorcycle. I was her "assigned" instructor. Rebecca was a nervous young woman whose feet barely touched the ground. She feared that the motorcycle would behave erratically, she would lose control of the vehicle, and it would throw her like a bucking bull.

On the first day, Gord, my fellow instructor, and I challenged the students with a noisy exercise and made them lean on the throttle to accelerate. The loud noise from the pit of those screaming 125 cc engines was enough to paralyze even the most courageous.

Gord and I next took the students through the gear-shifting exercise.

We taught the entire group, step by step, how to "open" the throttle and race down a straightaway in first gear.

With the concepts fresh in their minds, the students lined up with their motorbikes and took their turns "racing" in first gear down this runway. Rebecca "opened" her throttle, lurched, and stalled. She started the bike, "opened" her throttle again, lurched, and stalled again. I helped her to remember the lesson on "gradually releasing" the clutch.

She tried again and failed.

I reiterated a few of the key items.

She tried again and failed again.

I called Gord over to help us. When he stepped in and repeated the same information I had just given Rebecca, she suddenly "got" it.

With a different messenger, the information was successfully imparted and acted upon. This time, when she "opened" her throttle, she took off down the straightaway without any problem. The rest of the students cheered, and each time she repeated the stretch, she increased her speed, and her confidence grew.

The difference for Rebecca was not the information imparted, for Gord and I both were highly professional instructors. The difference was in how the teacher relayed the information and the context of what the student needed to hear. I was not the right teacher for her. Had she been able to select her "team," Gord would be in and I would be out.

Your selection is not a judgment of a person's caliber; rather, it is a reflection of communication styles and compatibility. Like tends to learn best from like. We most easily emulate those who reflect our own beliefs, who share our talents, and whose body language best mirrors ours.

When you choose people to work with you, to guide you, and to teach you, I suggest that you cast a wide net and then choose wisely.

I have become very intentional in selecting the people in my network.

My mentors must:

- be *exactly* where I intend to be in my future.
- mirror my talents.
- believe in my ability to learn from them
- understand that I plan to catapult beyond what they have taught me.

The people in my network must:

- support my purpose.
- complement my talents.
- have a shared interest in supporting my achievement, one that offers them a win as well.

The people in my mastermind group must:

- have shared visions of growth.
- challenge my talents and beliefs.
- have a need for personal growth and success.

The most valuable lesson I have learned from the twenty or so teachers I have studied with in the last decade is that I must focus on my particular talent and delegate everything else to others who have complementary strengths.

Yes, education matters. It *must* be a lifelong commitment for anyone seeking success, and myriad teachers are out there. Each mentor may promise the fruit of success, and each will have her own success stories. Carefully select the few from whom you are most likely to learn.

When you are looking for a mentor, look for someone who has *learned it, loves it,* and *lives it*:

- They've learned it. You want someone who has learned what you want to know. They may have a concrete skill (such as record keeping or firing practices) or a sideways or parallel skill (such as listening to their intuition when hiring a bookkeeper).

- They love it. You want someone who loves what she is doing, not a person who bemoans how much she hates her job. You want to learn from someone who is passionate about her work and her life.

- They live it. Her life is a true reflection of her learning, skills, passion, and achievements.

CONSIDER LEARNING FROM THOSE YOU ENVY

Envy is defined as an emotion that "occurs when a person lacks another's [perceived] superior quality, achievement, or possession and either desires it or wishes that the other lacked it."[38] In other words, it comes from a perceived lack that results from comparison.

Think of the phrase "keeping up with the Joneses." The Joneses have something that their near-peers consider to be important. Near-peers desire that "something" in order to have equal status. The closer you are in status, the more envy you may feel toward the person who has something you don't have.

Bertrand Russell notes that envy is one of the most potent causes of unhappiness.[39] Not only are people envious of other people's possessions and other status symbols, but our negative mindset may also drive us to rob others of their good fortune or to desire that some misfortune befall them.

Although envy is generally seen as something negative, I propose that envy can also be a constructive driving force.

Let's take "annual income earned" as a measurable. Who might you envy in the list below?

- A member of the British Royal Family
- A member of the Rockefeller or Rothschild family
- The prime minister or president of your country
- A business person on the Fortune 500 list
- An owner of a business earning over $1 million annually
- A CEO earning $500,000 annually
- A network marketer earning $300,000 annually
- A director earning $85,000 annually
- A manager earning $35,000
- An employee earning $25,000
- A writer earning an income from her writing
- An author earning an income from her book
- A painter earning an income from her art
- A musician earning an income from her music
- A songwriter earning an income from her lyrics
- A network marketer earning $10,000 annually from a second job
- An entrepreneur who has quit a job and is pursuing her life-long dream
- A person who just got fired
- An unemployed person
- A homeless person fishing food out of the garbage

Who you envy is an indication of what is there for you to achieve, what is within your realm of possibility.

Notice that you are not envious of people whose status is at a level that you consider impossible for yourself. For instance, if being the head of the royal family is not likely in your future, you probably won't feel envious of the person who might acquire that role.

Shift your attention toward those you do envy. Maybe you envy an entrepreneur, or a director or manager. I suspect that whoever ends ups on your envy list has achieved something you subconsciously know you are capable of achieving.

Like the person who thinks she is infinitely lucky, you can perceive envy as something that's dark and negative or as inspiration—something your subconscious believes you can achieve.

> *Envy is pointing out your own personal glass ceiling. Envy is your subconscious mind screaming out to you that this is entirely within your realm of possibility. Embrace you inner glass ceiling, and strive to shatter it.*

Envy is not a bad-news indicator that reflects something awful about you. Rather, it is a great-news indicator, telling you that you too can achieve this particular aspiration. All you have to do is to step out of your comfort zone and start moving toward it.

One of the best ways to beat this emotion is to meet with the person you envy.

Find out from that person what her beliefs are, how she acts, and what she did to get where she is. A person who has achieved what you consider to be a great goal has established a formula that has worked for her. In Neurolinguistic Programming circles, learning from someone who has succeeded is known as modeling. It's now up to you find out what the formula is to model.

CALL TO ACTION

Make a list of people who are of equal or higher status that you envy. Make a list of what they specifically have or do that you desire. Think of that promotion you should have had. Think of that technological gadget your neighbor just bought that you can't afford. Think of that vacation your sibling took that was out of this world.

I am envious of _____.

I am envious because this person has/is/does/owns (etc) _____
_____
_____
_____

This envy shows me that I can have/be/do/own (etc.) _____
_____
_____
_____

What small (ninety-second) step can I take today to move myself closer to attaining something I envy? _____
_____
_____
_____

I am grateful this person is in my life because _____
_____
_____
_____

Chapter 6

MAKING MEANINGFUL CONNECTIONS

When people hear the term, "networking," apprehension is typically the first response. Our first assumption is often that it means speaking with strangers. This apprehension is actually very common. It's a social phobia akin to public speaking.

We've often heard that public speaking ranks as the highest fear among humans, with the fear of death ranking as second.

Public speaking is a form of social phobia. Social phobia is essentially stage fright, whether you are on a stage or not. It's a fear of being criticized by others, of being judged and condemned. You need not be on a stage to feel this fear. Walking into a room full of strangers can also trigger a manifestation of this social phobia.

Nor are you alone in feeling this fear. A recent article in the *New York Times* notes that social phobia (also known as social anxiety) as a psychiatric condition is on the rise, going from 1.7% of the population in 1984 to 6.8% in 2005. That's an impressive 400% increase over two decades![40] When it exists as a psychiatric condition, rest assured

> *The statistics on sanity are that one out of every four Americans is suffering from some form of mental illness. Think of your three best friends. If they're okay, then it's you.*
> — **Rita Mae Brown**

that many of us have this same phobia, although not in a life-paralyzing way.

People with a psychiatric social phobia are at one end of the continuum. At the other end are the extroverts who recharge with new audiences. Most of us range somewhere in between, dealing with mild discomfort in social situations to extreme shyness manifesting itself in the form of a wallflower at social functions.

Understanding the different ways we can make meaningful connection is critical to your success. Yes, there is cold networking where you walk into a room of strangers and set out to explore potential partnerships by opening your mouth and doling out your business cards. But other ways exist for building your networks, extending your reach, and connecting with people.

In this chapter, we are going to focus on the different ways we can build connections, be it through networks, mentors, or mastermind groups. If you fear it, you should do it. But if it inspires internal dread, then perhaps you need to work your way up to it. Walking into a room filled with strangers is only one way to grow your support base. Perhaps you are relieved to hear there are other ways as well.

- **Networks** are open-ended avenues of support that you can call upon to propel your dream forward. A network typically presents ways to market and promote your business. You can build networks by continually making new connections (i.e., walking into a room of strangers). A network can also be a list of existing resources that help you to grow your business through access to specialized services (i.e., walking into a room of friends).

- **Mentors** are counselors, teachers, or trusted friends who are more experienced than you and have achieved some degree of success in your particular area of aspiration. Mentors guide you in your major purpose. Their guidance can be provided in person, through books, or through teleseminars and online courses.

- A **mastermind** group is a circle of people who meet regularly to support each member's primary projects. According to Napoleon Hill (reputed to have originated the term), a mastermind group comes together to coordinate both "knowledge and effort, in a spirit of harmony, between two or more people, for the attainment of a definite purpose."[41]

We'll begin with a closer look at building networks.

NETWORKS

When many of us hear the term, "networking," we immediately interpret it as "cold calling" and walking into a room full of strangers. Truth be told, there are those among us who would rather poke sticks into our eyes than walk into a room filled mostly with strangers, distribute our business cards, speak about our businesses, and "network."

Remember that old television commercial for Faberge Organic Shampoo? You tell two friends, and they'll each tell two friends, "and so on, and so on, and so on." That is word-of-mouth networking in action. It is like building a web of people who are energized by your idea, see its potential, and believe in it enough to share the news with some of their friends.

This—not the talking only to strangers—is the essence of networking. It can begin smoothly and easily, by talking with people you already know.

You only need to influence your immediate circle. Open a dialogue with them. Tell them your aspirations, and embrace their feedback until all parties are engaged and excited about the prospect. Are you launching a new product? Are you venturing out on your own? Are you seeking a promotion? Are you contemplating a career change? Yes, on your own you can set out to achieve your means. In good time. With a network of people supporting you and talking about your aspiration to others in a position to influence a maker or a shaker, your forward momentum will accelerate dramatically.

I'd rather you didn't poke your eye out! If you are one of the many who is uncomfortable with networking (with strangers), here's an exercise that will open your eyes to what is *already* available to you.

CALL TO ACTION

The following exercise is a list-generation exercise referencing your mental inventory of people you know, including your family, friends, colleagues, and neighbors. It also includes the people in your community with whom you do volunteer work, or whom you encounter in living your daily life (going grocery shopping, getting your hair cut, or catching the bus to work).

1. Which people in your immediate circle of friends and acquaintances do you know who have influence and power? What are their areas of expertise? Whom can they influence?

2. Who are the most specialized people you know? What technical abilities do they have, or what exclusive skills or services do they offer?

3. Considering the specialized people you have just listed, to what skill sets do you have access?

4. Who in your immediate circle of friends and acquaintances has access to a broader network than yours?

5. Consider all the people you have listed so far; think about all the other people to whom you have indirect access.

Keep your lists handy because you will find that over the next few days you will think of still more people to add to them.

Telling another person, even (or especially) someone you know, of your aspirations can be a daunting task. It will require you to step out of your comfort zone and risk criticism (we'll talk about this in Section Three). So why compound that discomfort by insisting that you need to network with strangers?

Meeting strangers will come as a natural part of networking through your friends—and they won't really be strangers but friends of friends. For instance, in writing this book, a friend of mine knew another author who had published a book. After discussing my venture with my friend, I decided it would be a good idea for me to meet with this author so I could learn from his trials and tribulations. Learning from someone else's errors is also known as "accelerated learning." Of course, from meeting with him, I learned a lot and saved myself from experiencing potential future frustration.

Knowing what you want (clarity), being open to opportunity, and believing in yourself will put you on an interesting path. Leveraging the support and interest of the people you already know and trust will help you travel your path at an accelerated rate.

Networking is all about building the foundation and framework from which you are going to operate. It is about connecting with the flesh-and-bones people in your life. The people in your network can have a skill set that works with, expands, or completes your own skill sets. They may have the money you don't have, the network you need, or the resources you would like to access.

Networking can be as tough or as easy as you make it out to be. I suggest taking the easy path first to build support and forward momentum. You can always ease yourself into the more difficult ways later, once your unstoppable journey has begun.

MEETING MINDFUL MENTORS

Mentors are a very specific group of people in your network. The bulk of your mentors can (and should) come from the networking lists you developed in the previous chapter.

You can receive mentoring in two different ways: a direct interpersonal exchange between you and another person with the desired expertise, or by remote exposure where the communication is one-way (from them to you). Each offers incredible value, and the application of *both* will expedite your growth.

Ultimately, a mentor is a wise and trusted counselor or teacher who can provide you with specific guidance.

Establishing a Direct Relationship with a Mentor

Many ways exist to establish a relationship with a live human being, so to simplify your selection process, let's put your potential mentors into two different categories. You can choose from the people who are familiar to you, or you can select a stranger, someone you don't know (yet). Whether you begin with someone who is familiar or unfamiliar to you is very much a personal choice. When I look at the personal mentors in my life, they are almost all in the unfamiliar category. For me, it was easier to enter into a business-like arrangement with someone with whom I had no personal business and with whom my discussions would be very focused and intentional. I liken it to seeing a counselor: I prefer the objective third person who is uninvolved in my life on a personal level.

Formal mentoring programs are common at some work places, at universities, and through government-sponsored and independent entrepreneurship programs. Begin by looking for these in your community.

If you prefer using the experts and professionals already known to you, start by looking at the information you gathered in the networking list. Start thinking about the people you know who have already made the journey upon which you are embarking.

Whether you are asking a familiar or an unfamiliar person to mentor you, you can approach the person in several different ways. The most simple and direct way is just to ask. This way is also the most emotionally risky as we tend to interpret a "no" as a direct rejection of our personal selves. But while the rejection might be hard to handle (due to our frequent "misinterpretation" of what was actually being rejected), an acceptance can be an incredibly joyful event. Another way is to offer a trade, either by way of bartering a trade of skills or by paying cold hard cash. This approach is less emotionally risky because we can interpret a "no" as a rejection of the transaction.

Just Ask

The fear that stops many people from approaching a mentor is, as we discussed earlier, self-deprecation. We can all too easily believe our own negative self-chatter: "Why would she want to help me? Why would she want to work with me? She has so much experience and I'm still floundering. She'll think I'm stupid."

Let's turn this around. Have you ever been asked for help? Have you ever been approached by someone at work, at school, or at home who needs help with a project or a task? Think about what *your* response has been.

I typically bend over backward to help others. I admire them for having the courage to ask. I am honored that they see me as an expert, and I typically give more than I've been asked to give.

Have you ever helped anyone, with or without being asked?

It makes you feel good, doesn't it?

If you have helped others, and felt great about offering that help, wouldn't it be nice to give somebody the opportunity to feel just as great about herself?

You may find yourself in a situation where you want to ask for someone's guidance or mentorship, but you're terrified to ask her. If you marshal your courage and just ask, you may be surprised to receive a "yes" answer as I did when approaching a potential advisor in graduate school.

When I started working on my Master's Degree in English Literature at Memorial University of Newfoundland, I signed up for all the courses except the one on the Renaissance. As an undergraduate, I had struggled for a C in Shakespeare. I felt that Renaissance English was too hard to read and had no relevance in today's world, and I saw no point in subjecting myself to another low grade.

I wanted to concentrate my efforts on the writings of contemporary Canadian authors. I knew the field well, and I felt it held some relevance in the world.

I made a point of hanging out in the grad lounge prior to the beginning of class. I was starting the program late in the year (winter semester), and I wanted to find out how the students' felt about the professors.

I found out that the best and most engaging professor in the program was Dr. Bill Barker. "You absolutely *must* take a course with him," I was told. Lucky for me, he was teaching a graduate class that semester. You guessed it—he taught the Renaissance course, which that year was focusing on Edmund Spenser's *The Faerie Queene*.

After hearing his praises from a few more grad students, I decided to go against my own advice and dump my Contemporary Canadian Lit class in favor of Dr. Barker's class.

It was a night class, Monday evenings from 7pm to 10pm.

The students were right; Professor Bill Barker was an absolute gem. We came into our first class, and instead of having the glare of the ceiling's neon bright white lights, Dr. Barker had placed four lamps in each corner of the room. So, already, we had ambiance. And when I made my first in-class joke (how obviously cliché it was that Saint George followed

Una's ass), his already sparkling eyes laughed along with everyone else in the class.

It didn't take me long to develop an academic interest in the man. It was clear he was intelligent and passionate about his topic, and secure enough to be playful with the subject matter. He breathed life into a dead text as far as I was concerned, and I absolutely loved the magical light that was ever-present in this man's eyes.

Sure enough, when the course came to its inevitable end, I was determined not to let this man's brilliance, coupled with his *joie-de-vivre* and the twinkle in his eye, slip away from me.

That's right; I decided to pop the question.

I remember screwing up all my courage before going to his office to ask whether he would work with me as my advisor as I completed my thesis. I was scared that he would say no, but I was determined to do what was within my power to secure this man as my thesis supervisor. I knew that if I didn't ask, the only guarantee was that it wouldn't happen; if I did ask, it might.

I went to see him in his office and held my hands on my lap to stop them from betraying my nervousness.

"Dr. Barker," I began, "Um, well, I was wondering whether you would be my thesis supervisor."

He looked me in the eye and said, "Sure."

And that was it. It really was that easy! I proceeded to tell him what my idea was, and we set up an appointment to iron out the details. With Dr. Barker's mentorship, guidance, and intellectual input, I completed my courses, wrote my thesis, and graduated.

I have since applied the same direct approach in seeking other mentors in life. It's not always been that easy or that successful. Indeed, I have more rejections under my belt than successes. But those relationships I have pursued and achieved through the simple (and terrifying) act of asking have been the lifeblood of my life's journey so far.

The experience has taught me a great life lesson about asking for help and finding mentors to guide you. Successful people ask for help.

Just ask.

Trade Your Skills

When I first started to think about online marketing strategies, I knew I was out of my element. Marketing was not my forte—online marketing even less so.

I focused on my strength (organizing chaos from a big-picture viewpoint) and decided to trade it for the knowledge of someone already successful in the online marketing field from whom I could learn.

I stumbled upon Ronnie Nijmeh, owner and operator of PLR.me. He had successfully implemented a monthly membership site, and I wanted to learn his list-building, search engine ranking, and online marketing strategies.

After I offered to trade him eighty hours of work for the opportunity to pick his brain, wonderful things happened. Ronnie wanted me go through a giant jumble of miscellaneous notes and turn them into a comprehensive report. To me, it was an easy project. I didn't have to write much original content, just organize existing material. I finished the work in about forty hours.

Ronnie was so impressed with my work that he featured me on one of his mastermind calls as a Documentation Specialist, which gave me additional exposure and allowed me to establish my expertise with a new audience.

Our trade of talents was a win-win for both of us as well as for our respective clients.

You, too, now have a sense of where your talents lie, and you know how valuable they are to others. What can you access through negotiation? How can people benefit from knowing you, as you benefit from knowing them?

Buy Their Time

When I first conceived the idea for this book, I knew I had a message I wanted to deliver: I could change lives, and I could be of service to many. But the thought of sitting down and writing a 200+ page book was daunting. The largest document I had ever written was my thesis, which was about 125 pages.

Then, one day, I attended an event that featured a presenter named Patrick Snow, the author of the bestseller *Creating Your Own Destiny: How to Get Exactly What You Want Out of Life.*

Prior to the presentation, some of the coordinating staff members whom I knew personally approached me and said how I would really like this speaker. I made a point of hunting Patrick Snow down before he gave his talk. Not yet knowing the name of his book, I introduced myself to him, saying, "I've been told that it is my destiny that I meet you; that means it's also your destiny to meet me. My name is Britt Santowski and...." I told him who I was (an entrepreneur and small business coach) and what I was doing (wanting to write a book).

By the end of the day, I had faxed him my credit card billing information, and a very solid and lucrative business partnership was achieved. Patrick became my Publishing Coach, and it was through him that I developed the highly skilled team that supported the growth and development of this book, from editors to cover designers and from to publishers to professionals skilled in marketing techniques. The result of this collaboration is now what you hold in your sweet hands.

So whether you ask for your mentor's help, trade services with him or her, or buy the person's time, your flexibility and persistence will equal your success.

Remote Mentors

Remote mentors are people with whom you may not have direct or individual contact. You can be remotely mentored by the authors of books you read, by courses you take, by attending seminars, and by joining select online networks.

Remote mentors are by far the easiest relationships since only minimal effort is required from you. Read the book, take the course, show up, and be open to learning.

Books

I'm proud to say that we are a very literate society! About half of Americans surveyed in a 2005 Gallop poll are reading about five books per year.[42] Books are a form of mentorship as you are following the particular teachings of an expert you have heard of (by word-of-mouth), or whose book you've randomly encountered while perusing the shelves at the bookstore or library. Often once you find the mentor, you will go on to read many of his or her books.

Courses

You can take courses from a number of places, beginning with at your workplace (if that's an option) or within your local community. Many schools and colleges offer special interest courses taught by local experts. It's a great way to meet local mentors as well as to network with like-minded people, in person, face-to-face. And there's also a plethora of free offerings online if you just skim the surface of the Internet. Many of these courses are intended to develop marketing leads for more in-depth and more expensive courses, but you can definitely learn a lot skimming the surface of free.

Seminars

The self-help seminar industry is booming in North America. It's easily a multi-billion dollar industry[43] with courses ranging in price from free (for the introductory session, which can be up to four days long) to $30,000. The self-help industry is unregulated, so it's a case of buyer beware. Recently, a personal-development seminar went incredibly wrong, and three people died at a sweat lodge retreat run by James Arthur Ray, a prominent self-proclaimed self-help guru.

Most seminars, however, are not death traps. There is a pattern, though, of extreme euphoria and optimism and possibility for people while in the actual seminar, which then ebbs at a rate that increases exponentially with every passing day after the seminar. Also, because these guru-led seminars are held only a few times a year in the bigger cities, the chances of creating a meaningful and long-term connection with other seminar attendees is greatly reduced compared to attending something in your own community. (I discuss the self-help phenomenon in greater detail in Chapter 8: The (F)Law of Attraction; it's buyer-beware out there!.)

I encourage you to attend local seminars first. Pay tuitions that are in the hundreds, not the thousands. Or attend free seminars and leave your credit cards and check books at home. Better yet, find the free seminars offered by your local business bureau or your place of employment.

But most importantly, do your homework! Research the seminar team and the organization behind it. Find others who have attended the seminar and ask how the seminar impacted their long-term development of their own personal pursuits.

Online Networks

Online networks are the final remote mentoring vehicle available to you. These networks are rapidly growing in number, and they can be found through your social networks, discussed in greater detail in the following chapter.

With the Internet growing at an explosive rate, you need to start establishing meaningful filters. Typically, these can be through blogs of like-minded individuals, or through membership-driven sites.

- Mommy Millionaire, a women's-only entrepreneur networking space founded by Kim Lavine. (www.mommymillionaire.com)

- Femalepreneurs, a site that offers to teach women how to find a niche and make it fun and profitable (www.femalepreneurs.com/blog)

- Startup Princess, a blog that besides having a great name promotes growth and success for female entrepreneurs (www.startupprincess.com)

- Entrepreneur Journey Blog, a blog that offers incredible information for bloggers and online marketers. (www.entrepreneurs-journey.com)

Making the Final Selection

Ultimately, you want to find a mentor who has traveled your path, one who understand the trials and tribulations you will face in your undertakings. The following story illustrates the importance of finding a mentor suited to your personality, needs, and goals.

A mother walked many miles to visit Gandhi and ask for help with her little girl. She asked, "Please Bapu, tell my little girl to stop eating sugar. She simply eats too much sugar and will not stop." Gandhi told the mother to leave and come back with the girl in a month.

The mother returned with her child in a month, and again she asked, "We have come back as you asked. Please tell my little girl to stop eating sugar."

Gandhi turned to the girl and said, "Young child, stop eating sweets. They are not good for you."

The mother asked Gandhi, "Bapu, why didn't you say that when we first came to see you? Why did you ask us to leave and come back in a month? I don't understand."

Gandhi replied, "I asked you to return with the girl in one month, because one month ago, I, too, was eating sweets. I could not ask her to stop eating sweets if I had not stopped doing so."

When you're looking for a mentor, find somebody who possesses the qualities, skills, and experiences you hope to have yourself. Look for individuals who share your values—the greater the alignment of your values, the better the relationship will be. An ideal mentor will be someone who fits your idea of success, has a positive and encouraging attitude, and openly shares her knowledge and her experiences with you.

You can consider a mentor at the height of her success within her profession, or you can choose someone who is traveling the same path as you but is several steps ahead of you. This type of relationship will bring you a greater sense of immediacy, will challenge you to learn from your failures, and will spark solutions that can benefit both of you.

Even if your mentor anticipates sharing her knowledge with you without much in return, she will in fact grow from the experience. The ideal mentoring relationship will be one that improves the lives of both participants—a win/win.

Mastering Mastermind Groups

Now that you have made your lists of networking resources and potential mentors, it's time to consider developing or joining a mastermind group. A mastermind group is a regular meeting of two or more people who agree to provide unlimited support to the fullest of their abilities to each other's pursuits. They have full and unconditional faith in the other members' talents and abilities. Masterminding is based on the idea that when two or more people coordinate in a spirit of harmony, and help each other work toward a definite objective or purpose, they absorb and magnify each other's creative power and results.

An authentic, highly supportive mastermind group is one of the most powerful tools available to you. A good mastermind group will propel you to heights previously unimagined.

Mastermind groups are discussed in Napoleon Hill's famous book *Think and Grow Rich*. Hill learned of the concept from Andrew Carnegie who had successfully used mastermind groups to build his steel business.

The greatest self-made millionaires and billionaires have participated in mastermind groups:

- Andrew Carnegie, J.P. Morgan, and John Rockefeller
- Thomas Edison, Henry Ford, and Harvey Firestone
- The Wright Brothers
- Bill Gates and Paul Allen
- Jack Canfield and Mark Victor Hansen

The magic behind the mastermind group is personal-growth-focused brainstorming. Where career-based brainstorming typically focuses on a work-related problem, a mastermind group focuses entirely on *you*. When creative minds meet and unite, amazing ideas are born.

Definition of the Mastermind Group

Let's explore mastermind groups in greater detail. In *Think and Grow Rich*, Hill writes that there are essentially three sources of knowledge:

- Infinite Intelligence: Creative imagination combined with the field of information.
- Accumulated Experience: What you already know and have already learned, whether formally or informally.
- Experiment and Research: The continuing "school of knowledge" being carried out every day in the world around you.

According to Hill, the mastermind group is a source of inspiration that goes far beyond the capabilities of individual effort. Indeed, Hill states, "No two minds ever come together without, thereby, creating a third, invisible, intangible force which may be likened to a third mind."[44]

Mastermind groups are planned and regular brainstorming. Everyone in the group benefits from the experience, the resources, and the explosion of ideas and solutions that inevitably arise.

To each mastermind participant, you give your whole and undivided individual attention; in return, you receive a multitude of ideas and feedback from the group.

Top Benefits of Participating in a Mastermind Group

When you participate in a mastermind group that is genuinely interested in and committed to your success, you might expect to receive the following:

- You will be in an environment that supports your growth.

- You will have the encouragement of people who are committed to moving your business or project forward and who are committed to seeing you succeed.

- You dramatically increase your chances of reaching your goals, as this group of people will help you to brainstorm solutions and take action.

- You will be held accountable. The other group members will hold you to your commitments.

- You will have more fun while others cheer you on to greater results. They'll help you when you fall, rally for you when you're moving forward, and celebrate with you when you succeed.

- You will get helpful feedback, and you can bounce any idea off the members before you implement it, thereby saving yourself time, energy, and money.

- You will find solutions to problems from proactive, objective people who want you to succeed.

- You will benefit from the self-mastery and leadership skills you will acquire as you support and coach each other within the group. You will develop an unstoppable belief in yourself and your abilities.

- You will be a part of something special, even magical. You will feel the positive charge in the inspired undertakings that come out of each meeting, and you will harness an unlimited source of group synergy.

- You will develop deep and meaningful relationships with successful, like-minded people and, through them, dramatically expand your network.

Several ways exist to get involved in a mastermind group. First, you can "buy" a seat in one. A friend of mine, Melanie Norris of Freshleafdesign.com (who is the designer of the Cushion Corset), explored this option. She had done some online research and found a women's mastermind group. Melanie expressed an interest in joining, and the women extended an invitation to her. She was shocked to learn that the group charged $17,000 for an annual membership.

A mastermind group supports all of its members unconditionally and with unwavering faith. While money can buy a membership, it cannot buy genuine interest. I advocate joining a group where you know the other person or people or at least have received a word-of-mouth recommendation for it.

The first thing to do when starting a group is to find the right people. Our tendency is to cluster around people who are like us, in the same income range, and with the same interests. For a mastermind group to work, you need to include people who are *not* like you but who still support you and your vision.

Reach up. Find people who have already achieved what you aspire to or something similar. Then reach out. Find people whose strengths complement rather than duplicate yours. If you want to write a book, for example, find someone who has authored a book, and find people with networks larger than yours. Then find someone in publishing and someone else in education or public speaking.

Limit the group's size. My first mastermind group launched my career as an educator and coach for women. I co-founded the group with a woman who was both my "reach up" person and who had a network larger than mine. We each invited three other women, expecting that at least a few would decline, but none did! With a group of eight, we had to be very precise with our timekeeping and meeting structure.

As the years progressed, a few women stepped out of the group, and a few more were invited to join. The group stabilized at six members, which was a more manageable number.

For the past several years, I've also established a one-on-one mastermind relationship with my mentor and trainer, Paul Thompson. We meet on a weekly basis to support each other in our writing and professional training careers.

The effective and dedicated mastermind group really is a central key to accelerated growth.

Your Mastermind Group

Have set guidelines for how the group will function so it can meet its goals and purpose. Below are guidelines I have developed over three years of working with mastermind groups. Whenever I start or am asked to start a group, I begin with the guidelines. I then get the group to refine its tenets to meet its members' particular needs.

Suggested Guidelines

Invite givers from whom you can grow. Reach up and over. Invite others who complement your skills instead of mirror them. In other words, create good company and be in good company.

Coordinate in the spirit of harmony. Complaining, whining, arguing, or negating ideas are not welcome. Gossip is out-and-out banned. Gently remind people to express positive solutions.

I've found that the optimal group size is five to seven members due to time constraints (with eight or more, it is difficult to give individualized attention).

The roles of the facilitator and timekeeper are rotated. A meeting cycle is considered complete when everyone has had an opportunity to facilitate the group. After each cycle, the group's guidelines and memberships are modified as necessary.

Members should miss no more than two meetings per cycle, as the group depends on receiving your input as much as you depend on the rest of the group. (Members who miss more than two meetings per cycle may be asked to leave the group to allow for another person to join.) If a member is unable to attend in person, she may attend via a conference call.

Each member should be supported verbally and emotionally. The group principle is that we can believe for others what they cannot fully believe for themselves. These are not idle words. Each member is honor-bound to support her fellow group members, and as such, believe in each member's ability to pursue and achieve her dreams. You will also enjoy the feeling of being fully supported by the group.

My current group meets twice each month. We have a predetermined time and location, and we follow a preplanned agenda. We start and finish on time, and ask that participants arrive five minutes before the designated start time. Latecomers are asked to enter quietly and join the existing flow of the conversation. Time waits for no one; neither do we.

Our meetings run like a Swiss watch. We have committed to a ninety-minute session and we keep within that timeframe. The group facilitator and timekeeper play important roles: The facilitator keeps the conversation on track; the timekeeper rations each person's airtime and participation. Have a watch or stopwatch available.

Below is the template that we use in our mastermind group.[45] The timeline represented below is the one that works for our group. Your timeline will depend on the size of your group, and the agreements made by your members.

Step 1: Open with an inspirational quotation

Our group begins each meeting with the facilitator reading an inspirational piece from a book she is reading or a meaningful quote she has encountered. This step is an excellent way to dip into the mind of the facilitator, as well as to expand your reading list.

Step 2: Share what's new

Do a round table of good news. You can share a positive outcome of a current project or an event. Begin the meeting by celebrating successes and establishing a positive mindset. If someone is unsure what to say, she can use a scripted, "Last meeting I said I would _____, and then I did _____." Each person is allotted one minute.

Step 3: Negotiate for time

Before launching into the real purpose for the meeting, we always do a check in to see whether anyone needs extra time during the meeting. If so, another participant can forfeit her time so the extra time can be allotted to another member. We've used this process to deal with the occasional upsets that happen in this thing called Life.

Step 4: Round table of challenges

Participants have an allotted time to present a challenge and get feedback from the group. The longer you take to present your challenge, the shorter the time allowed for feedback. Conversely, the more succinct you are, the greater the time allowed for feedback. In our group, we let each person choose whether she wants to do it in a more formal, round-table format, or whether she would prefer a "brainstorming dump" where solutions are put forward as they are conceived. In another group I was in, we did only the round-table. The format will depend on the group.

Step 5: Commitments

The round table is then followed with a quick "Commitment to Stretch." Each member commits to complete a specific task by the next meeting. An example would be committing to making two cold calls, committing to meeting someone you admire, or committing to an event that puts you outside your comfort zone. This step is where you commit to action and are held accountable by the group.

One group I knew about had a few members that would commit and never follow up. On collaborative agreement, the group instituted a significant "fine" that would be payable if a commitment made to the mastermind group was not completed. This served two purposes: First, it instilled a direct consequence for unmet promises; second, it inspired the mastermind group to commit with care. Over-promising and under-delivering skidded to a stop once this measure was introduced.

Step 6: Announcements

This part of the meeting is for announcements of upcoming events and networking.

Depending on the length of the meeting, you may decide to have a "free for all" period at the end, at which time anyone can have a chance to speak.

Other Mastermind Tips

I consider these following items to be critical to any mastermind group's success:

- Meet regularly, such as the second and fourth week of each month.

- There is no such thing as a bad idea; don't make anybody wrong. As soon as you begin attacking the creativity of the group, ideas will shrivel up. Keep the brainstorming going, and you'll be astounded at the levels of insight you reach.

- Treat each meeting as if you actually paid $17,000 a year to be a member. A mastermind meeting isn't an opportunity to catch up on gossip and old friends. It can only be effective if all members take it seriously. Show up ready to focus, prepared to give, and open to receive.

- Hold one another accountable. Know your goals. Know when you expect to achieve them. Your mastermind team wants to know, and there is great power in verbalizing your intention.

- Create an agenda and stick to it! Excellent moderation skills come in handy here, as does a timer that actually beeps.

Your mastermind group will allow you to benefit deeply from the collaborative process while giving back to each member. Once you have joined or set up a mastermind group, you will find that your network naturally expands, you will increase your access to mentors, and your opportunities for success will grow exponentially.

Chapter 7

COLLABORATION TOOLS

We can work and live in our existing circle of connections, or we can leverage the rich world of experience that exists beyond our immediate bubble, through all the people that are continually surrounding us. The existing circle option is often the most comfortable, because it means we can stay nicely nestled within our existing relationships. Which is nice, if you want to stay exactly where you are today. But I'm assuming you want to grow, which is why you are reading this book.

All collaboration begins with identifying and meeting people from whom you can grow. In the Networking section's Call to Action, you were called upon develop five extensive list of the people you could access in your life. If you haven't completed this section, you really should; if you did, it's now time to call it up.

MASTERING THE INTRODUCTION

A business-focused introduction consists of three critical components: your ability to state your name; a strong and effective handshake; and, when appropriate, concisely presenting your business.

> *The definition of insanity is doing the same thing over and over and expecting a different result.*
> — Attributed to Benjamin Franklin

Saying Your Name!

In one of her televised presentations, Suze Orman (a financial advisor for women) prompts a room full of women to say their individual names. A dull murmur involuntarily shudders through the room. Orman challenges the women to take pride in their names by each saying her FULL name strong and loud. After several rounds of serious prompting, the women strongly and articulately say their names. The dull murmur is replaced by a reverberating boom that proudly exclaims, "I am here! Look. It's *me*."

Your name is your label to the world. It is what the brain responds to most powerfully. It is the information that precedes you when you enter a room. It is what remains after you are gone.

Sometimes, however, women falter when it comes to introducing themselves. Whether because of the politics or conventions of names, we are often unable to speak our names with strength and conviction.

Your name, the one you use *right now*, needs to be spoken with strength and conviction each and every time you meet someone new. Men do it all the time without effort. Women, however, often let their voices go soft, or let their eyes drift aside, or say only their first names, or neglect saying their names altogether.

Get used to saying your name.

Initiating the Handshake

A handshake says a great deal about who you are. If you're putting a cold dead fish into another person's hand, the recipient will not know whether to grab ahold of it, kiss it, or drop it. Likewise, if you clasp the other person's hand so hard that you hurt the other person, she or he will not be impressed.

Think of the handshakes you have received. If none come to mind, perhaps you haven't shaken enough hands.

Granted a bit of gender confusion is out there. When winners of the academy awards are received on stage, a man is greeted with a handshake or possibly a man-hug (one second shoulder-to-shoulder embrace coupled with a mutual pat-on-the-back) whereas the women are more typically greeted with a hug and possibly a kiss on the cheek. Social situations often mirror that norm.

Whereas the handshake is met in the male domain at every opportunity (business, social or close-personal) in our western world, women draw a range of physical welcomes, from a handshake (business) to a hug (social) to a kiss (close-personal).

Men and women alike share this confusion associated with greeting a woman. Many don't know whether a woman wants the handshake or a hug (the kiss is usually self-evident). You should therefore initiate the handshake yourself.

Historically, a handshake was used to show that both people were unarmed. Today, it is a critical gauge of confidence, trust, sophistication, and mood. Men typically shake hands more frequently than women. In business, handshaking is expected of everyone.

The way you shake someone's hand reveals a lot about you. A grip of steel can be seen as a desire to control; a limp, dead-fish grasp is a sign of insecurity or a lack of confidence. Mechanical, incessant pumping suggests mental rigidity, strong will, and inflexibility.

I still meet many women (and yes, even the occasional man) who opt for the dead-fish handshake, and I still find it off-putting. When greeted with a firm handshake from another woman, I delight in the prospect of getting to know her better. When a child gives me a limp handshake, I take the opportunity to challenge her or him to grasp my hand with firmness and strength.

A firm handshake, direct eye contact, an easy introduction, and a smile all help you to connect more dynamically with the other person.

Mastering Your Business Blurb

Stating your name and initiating the handshake are the key openers. Your job then is to find out more about the person you've had the good fortune to meet. As Epictetus once so famously said, "We have two ears and one mouth so we may listen more and talk the less."[45] Remember the self-described lucky people? This is where they find some of their opportunities.

What you do only matters to your listener if it personally relates to them. Ever met that person at a gathering who knew only how to talk about themselves? That person who never listened to what was important to you? After the introductions, listen. Inquire. Say that person's name back to them at least once. Remember, that is the sweetest sound in the world to them. Find out more about the other person. If your business, your skills or your passions can assist the other person in any way, then it is worth mentioning. If not, then you are just blowing empty air in their general direction.

Should the opportunity arise, should your skills and talent provide meaning to the other person, then you need to share it with them. Begin small. Do you help people write books? follow their dreams? ride motorcycles? train mice?

If they are interested in what you do, follow with a short description.

I help people write books by providing coaching and resources throughout the writing, production and the marketing stages.

You need to have a clear and concise summary of your business name, what you do, and what makes you different from others in your profession.

You want a tagline that has the ability to be noticed, to be remarkable. In his book, *Magical Worlds of the Wizard of Ads*, Roy H. Williams talks about the part of the brain's frontal lobe known as the Broca area. According to Williams, this area determines what gets (and stays) in cognition and what never enters. The Broca area is stimulated when *some auditory sounds* out of the ordinary are heard. Williams goes on to say that "the toll required at Broca's tollbooth is surprise—specifically, unpredictable words in unusual combinations."[46] The world's best performer of this skill is Dr. Seuss. Using rhyme and unexpected words that nevertheless carry meaning to the listener, Dr. Seuss created stories filled with words that can easily be memorized and recited by a child as young as five.

From the wonderful world of advertising, here are some of the big guns:

- GLAD Garbage Bags: "Don't get mad, get GLAD."
- Disneyland: "The happiest place on earth."
- Kellogg's Frosted Flakes: "They're gr-r-reat!"
- Miller Beer: "It's Miller time!"
- Energizer batteries: "It keeps going, and going, and going...."
- Kentucky Fried Chicken: "No one does chicken like KFC."
- Whisk Laundry Detergent: "Ring around the collar."

All these tips and well and good, but your best bet is to have your taglines, infomercial, business name and business cards all nicely tucked in your back pocket, ready to be called upon when needed. First and foremost, though, is to let the other person be your guide to their needs.

Speak once; listen twice.

Understanding the Stages of Group Dynamics

No matter what their size, all groups go through stages of development. One model of group development is known as "Forming, Storming, Norming, and Performing," to which I would like to add a fifth stage of developing, "Transforming."

Stage 1:   Forming (Getting Together). When your mastermind group first assembles, you will go through a process of getting settled. As with our first group, we spent the first eight weeks settling on a process that would carry us through the next few years. At the start, you will spend your time:

- Setting the ground rules
- Involving the right people
- Deciding to act
- Excited about the prospect of change and possibility

Stage 2:   Storming and Positioning—Building Trust and Establishing Shared Ownership. At this stage, relationships are formed. You have set the guidelines; you're now implementing them. You are getting to know each other in a deeper and more meaningful way. Conflicts may arise, and they will be ironed out. In this stage, you will be:

- Positioning
- Re-organizing chaos
- Identifying and revising ground rules
- Committing to collaborate
- Defining a collective vision as well as your individual goal
- Developing a base of common knowledge
- Engaging the other participants

Stage 3: Norming (Working within the Established Rules and Guidelines). Once the forming and storming have settled, you will find that the group establishes a rhythm or a momentum of its own. You know what's expected of you, you are beginning to know some of the other participants' inner workings, and you work with greater ease within your group. You now shift to a bigger picture and begin:

- Feeling greater stability, with everyone settling into her role.
- Developing more extensive and expansive plans of action.
- Examining and selecting specific strategies.
- Further developing your mission, your greater vision, your *raison d'être*.

Stage 4: Performing (Taking Action). The fourth stage happens when the group's momentum has been established, trust has been developed, and now momentum moves you full steam ahead. The ideas that are born and developed at the meetings inspire you in the lull between meetings. If you meet periodically, say every week or every second week, you find yourself inspired by the other participants' positive intentions when you move toward and fulfill your commitments. You are easily:

- Allowing all group members to interact and unfold.
- Adapting new ideas and expanding on past and existing ideas.
- Implementing plans of action.
- Acting on commitments and co-creating effortlessly.
- Formalizing interagency relationships that grow from the group and reach beyond the group.

Stage 5: Transforming. In the positive environment you have now formed, the magic of synergy can actually take place through:

- Intuitive understandings.
- The expanding of ideas, contacts, and potential.
- The development of a "third" or "divine" mind that is a culmination of the "group think."
- Unlimited support in each other's growth.

In a negative environment, the group either disbands or segments, which in turn allows for the possibility of a new cycle to begin again.

In a positive environment, the collaborative culture has deepened within you, and you are now the full recipient of the full benefits offered through the mastermind process.

SUSTAINING ANY BENEFICIAL RELATIONSHIP

Once you have decided with whom you want to work, determine how you will approach her, him, or them. Here are a few tips:

- **Be as upfront as you can about your expected outcomes**. If you don't know what you want to get out of any relationship, it has little chance of success.

- **Take full responsibility**. Whether you are a junior, equal peer, or senior partner in any relationship, it is still your role to take the driver's seat. Articulate your expectations so that those working with you can provide you with what you need. Likewise, you need to listen to their expectations, so that you can meet their needs as well.

- **Stay focused on the positive**. With every upset comes a growth opportunity. Should anyone become more focused on the upsets, it is your job to re-focus on the learning opportunities.

- **Be honest**. All people respond to, and respect, honesty. When you feel inadequate, scared, or vulnerable, stating how you feel may bring surprising insights and much-needed support.

- **Apologize**. If you do anything that negatively affects or offends, apologize. Being able to admit when you're wrong and to apologize nurtures respect and strengthens your relationship.

- **Communicate regularly**. A trusting and nurturing relationship can only be developed through regular contact. Meeting face to face is always the best, and when that is not an option, commit to staying in touch by phone or videoconference.

- **Recognize your own accomplishments**. As you are there to help others grow, so too are they there to help you. Your growth, successes and accomplishments will be another's reward. Do not minimize your own achievements—celebrate them.

- **Take genuine interest in the feedback that others provide**. When someone makes a suggestion, act on it. When she gives you a lead, contact the lead. When she gives you constructive feedback, listen.

- **Ask questions**. Smart people ask questions in the perpetual pursuit of knowledge; not-so-smart people hide their ignorance behind all-knowingness.

- **Don't gossip**. Hold yourself up to a higher level. Grow on the merits of your success and not by drawing attention to another person's failure.

Participating in any interpersonal relationship is an incredible opportunity. Skilled people within your network can provide you with first-hand encouragement and advice. They either have already walked down the road you're on and already made mistakes they can teach you to avoid, or they have the skills you need to grow forward. They can save you a lot of time by directing you to the relevant and available resources that can best help you to achieve your dream.

More Networking Resources

A key launching pad for my career as a coach and motivational educator was Business Networking International. Dr. Ivan Misner, the "Father of Modern Networking," founded BNI in 1985. This impressive organization provides the basic tools of networking.

BNI gives you practical hands-on tools. While the focus is on internal networking within the existing branch, the skills you learn will help you in any networking situation. Their networking model centers entirely on word-of-mouth referrals. Word-of-mouth implies personal communication, which implies a network. If you are ready to network with your local businesses, I strongly urge you to find a BNI chapter near you.

One of the most valuable skills I learned with the BNI group is how to develop my own infomercial. Each BNI member is required to develop a thirty to sixty-second infomercial about his or her business. In the world of radio, a one-minute announcement is about eighty-five words.

Encapsulating your business in eighty-five words can be challenging.

When I was in university, I took an English course where I had to write four 1,000-word essays throughout the semester. I signed up thinking it would be a "bird" course (aka dead easy). After three years of writing ten to twenty-page essays, four pages should be simple.

However, I found that after years of developing an area of expertise and padding opinions with verbosity, thinning my opinion down to four pages was *much* harder than I had originally anticipated. I needed to be clear, concise, and to the point.

That is precisely what an eighty-five word, one-minute infomercial forces you to do.

In her book, *The Accidental Millionaire*, Stephanie Frank suggests you come up with a short (thirty-second), medium (five-minute) and longer (twenty-minute) infomercial. I recommend you begin by writing your longer version first, then pare it down, and pare it down again until just the bare bones are left.

Other models of in-person networking include the following:

- Your local Chamber of Commerce
- Networking organizations for female entrepreneurs
- Local and national business directories
- Local and national women's business networks
- Alumni networks

Social Networking

The new "social networking" includes building an online presence through sites such as MySpace, Facebook, Twitter, LinkedIn, and so on.

Online social networking has been compared to the Small World Phenomenon, also referred to as Six Degrees of Separation.[47] While the concept of social networking has existed since the mid-1950s, its reach, and hence its power, is only being realized today. We saw its power in gigantic proportions with its very successful deployment in Barack Obama's 2008 election strategy, a strategy that will be studied for years to come.[48] The power of social networking is just beginning to be realized, and this realization is going viral. With the development of global computer networks, almost-instantaneous access to anyone in the world is now a reality!

LinkedIn

LinkedIn is a network for professionals who wish to network with other likeminded professionals and who may be seeking employment opportunities. Created in 2003, LinkedIn now employs 385 staff members and hosts over 50 million members.

From the LinkedIn Web site, you learn the following:

- LinkedIn has over 50 million members in over 200 countries and territories around the world.
- A new member joins LinkedIn approximately every second, and about half of its members are outside the U.S.

- Executives from all Fortune 500 companies are LinkedIn members.[50]

LinkedIn emphasizes the importance of knowing your "Connections." If you are seeking an introduction to someone, the site helps you to contact the person, directly or through second- or third-degree connections). Like the BNI group, it's very much a referral-based system, where connection depends on getting personal referrals from people you know or who know of you.

Facebook

Facebook provides an excellent way to reconnect with your friends from the past. I'm in touch with people from decades ago, whom I thought I had long left behind. I'm also in touch again with the girls from my drink-till-you-drop days and am happy to hear that they have all flourished as interesting, vibrant, dynamic, and successful women. I've connected with the many interesting people with whom I hung out on the street, went to university with, and have worked with.

A regular Facebook page will accommodate as many as 5,000 "friends." If you want to keep track of more than 5,000 friends, you can build a fan page. With a fan page, you can also build a network of people who are interested in what you are doing and want to keep updated on your progress. These connections allow for an incredible networking opportunity.

Facebook has a number of applications that can be added in return for giving access permission to that particular application.

An excellent how-to-use-Facebook guide is available at the Mahalo Web site (www.mahalo.com/how-to-use-facebook).

There is nothing either good or bad, but thinking makes it so.
— William Shakespeare

Twitter

A friend of mine once summarized the difference between Facebook and Twitter by saying that Facebook is about the people you have known in the past, and Twitter is about hooking up with the people in your future.

Twitter has been referred to as a blog on steroids. Users are limited to 140 characters, and using this small space, they send out mini-updates to the online world. (While a Facebook account is not accessible until you accept someone's "friend request," Twitter posts are available for anyone online to see.)

One of my Twitter accounts has over 2,500 followers. A respectively impressive number, I agree, but none of the followers are substantive. Most of them are people eager to populate their "Tweet" empire. When they follow, the first thing they do is try to sell me something, or they want to give me something, in return for my registration. This online networking strategy is equivalent to approaching some stranger at a social gathering and thrusting your business card in his face along with an "invitation" to "join my database so I can keep you updated on this fabulous moneymaking opportunity."

Personally, I'd rather like to get to know the person first.

Another Twitter account I have has less than 100 people. These connections are more substantive, more meaningful.

Some resources that can enhance your tweet experience include the following:

- Twitter Style Guide as explained by Grammar Girl— http://grammar.quickanddirtytips.com/twitter-style-guide.aspx
- Twitter Glossary on the Twitter Fan Wiki— http://twitter.pbworks.com/Twitter+Glossary

- The Ten Rules of Twitter (and how the author Robert Scoble breaks everyone of them)—http://scobleizer.com/2007/09/23/the-10-rules-of-twitter-and-how-i-break-every-one

- Fifty ideas on how to use Twitter for business—http://www.chris-brogan.com/50-ideas-on-using-twitter-for-business

After this next Call to Action, it's time to put accountability and collaboration together to generate some significant, constructive and meaningful action in Section III on initiative.

CALL TO ACTION

Social networking can be a colossal waste of time, or it can be extraordinarily beneficial. Like anything, a tool in and of itself is neither good nor bad; what makes it so is how you use it. (A hammer is relatively useless when it comes to opening a bottle of Champagne, but incredibly capable of putting a nail into the wall to hang a picture.) Prior to setting up any social networking tool, ask yourself the following questions:

1. What is the purpose of this specific tool?

2. With whom do I intend to interact?

3. How will I reach this intended audience? You will want to pre-qualify your "friends" or "followers" (customers, networking leads, friends, future prospects, mentors, etc.)

4. Before getting started, do I have what I need to set up my site? (Appropriate avatar aka electronic image of yourself, resume, infomercial, etc.)

5. What, if known, are its time-wasters? (e.g. Facebook is cluttered with game applications; Twitter is flooded with irrelevant tweets about who ate what today.) Knowing the time-wasters lets you avoid them, so you can maximize your benefit.

These questions set the context that enables you to maximize the value of your social networking tools. If you already have pre-existing social networking tools, go through this process anyway. If you need to, you can re-vision your existing accounts, or you can establish new accounts. What's important is that these social networking tools work for you, not the other way around.

Section III

INITIATIVE

A Hard Decree

Last

Night

God
Posted
On the Tavern wall

A hard decree for all of love's inmates

Which read:

If your heart cannot find a joyful work

The jaws of this world
Will probably

Grab hold of your

Sweet

Ass

— **Hafiz,** *The Gift* (P. 212)

The first strategy revolved around accountability, and centered largely on the mindset of the individual. The second strategy touched on the mindset of woman-to-woman relationships, and then looked at the mechanics of collaboration. This third strategy is an amalgamation of both the mindset and mechanics of initiative.

Many people confuse initiative with action. Initiative includes action, but it is much more than that. Initiative is about being motivated to take the first step, even if it means stepping into unexplored territory. Initiative is the difference between the person who *sees* the potential in a situation and the person who *creates* potential.

Initiative is doing something not because you have been told to but because you want to. You need to. You have the drive, the ability, and the determination. Initiative is a mindset of success propelled by a vision or purpose that drives you to act. It is the process that can bring any idea into fruition. It is the driver; action is its child. Actions are the simple and single steps that are taken to turn this vision into a reality. The culmination of actions, propelled by initiative, are what make your dreams come true. While you should never underestimate the ***power*** of a single action, never underestimate the life-changing ***force*** of initiative.

Chapter 8

THE (F)LAW OF ATTRACTION

We're going to begin this third section with a look at the Law of Attraction. The Law of Attraction is a very popular and lucrative industry these days—mostly for the seminar leaders and occasionally for the student. In times of financial upheaval, the notion that we can "conceive, believe, and receive" exclusively through mental effort is especially appealing. Risk is minimal, as is the amount of action required, because it's all about your thoughts, we are promised. This message appeals to our fear (of poverty), greed (for money), and desire for ready access (the ease through which it is promised). The Law of Attraction is an idea currently generating a lot of money for those who are teaching it.

The Law of Attraction first became widely popular through Rhonda Byrne's 2006 hit movie, *The Secret*. The "secret," in a nutshell, is that if you can conceive it, you can receive it. Most of the movie's attention is about the importance of having the right thoughts; very little is given to the action required to make an event happen. From bicycles to sports cars, from illnesses to wealth, from physical and emotional abuse due to unpopularity to supreme marital bliss, it all begins and ends with what you are thinking.

While this movie is made out to unveil this so-called secret kept only by the rich of the world, the concept is not really that new. It has always been around, and it tends to fall into the limelight during times of financial crisis, like eras around recessions, depressions, and wartime.

James Allen spearheaded the literary explosion of this secret with his book *As a Man Thinketh* in 1902.[51] Wallace Wattles followed shortly after with a book called *The Science of Getting Rich* in 1910.

Dale Carnegie was also an early advocate of a person's ability to manifest her or his own reality, although he was one of the few who didn't tie it to the miracle of unlimited wealth. *How to Win Friends and Influence People* was one of the first best-selling self-help books when it was published in 1936. Napoleon Hill further popularized the concept in 1937 with his book *Think and Grow Rich*.

And in the post-war era where man struggled for his identity and quest for wealth, an era that saw the emergence of identity-crisis plays like Arthur Miller's *Death of a Salesman*, Earl Nightingale was one of the first to weave the concept into motivational speeches for sales representatives in the now-famous 1950 recording known as "The Strangest Secret."

Since 1986, we have the phenomenon of Esther and Jerry Hicks who call forth the spirit of Abraham. Channeled through Esther and communicating with Jerry, Abraham takes the time to provide mortals with divine instruction on effective thought management.

Contemporary teachers (often referred to as gurus) of thought-management are many. And because many profess to hold the secret to wealth (a direct manifestation of the proper application of thought), they may charge upwards to $10,000 per weekend seminar.

What all these sources are espousing is the "Responsibility Assumption," which is that you are the creator of your own life, and that you have anywhere from partial to substantial to total responsibility over what happens to you in your life.

THE FATAL FLAWS OF THE "LAW" OF ATTRACTION

According to those Law of Attraction proponents who believe you are entirely responsible for your own reality, anything you fear will come to pass. By intensely focusing on that fear, you give it the power to manifest itself into your life.

A fear I share with millions of others is the fear of flying. When I was younger, I was essentially fearless about anything. Flying was fun. And I loved the take-off and landing—until my mother told me (when I was old enough to "handle the truth") that those were indeed the most dangerous parts of the flight. And then I had a reason to be scared. Take-offs and landings ceased to be fun and instead become my most anxious parts of any flight.

When I watched the movie, *The Secret*, my fear of flying was renewed. Because, after all, as the Law of Attraction clearly states, what you think about is what you attract into your life.

Shortly after seeing this movie, and having been deeply impacted by it, I started becoming more and more aware of my thoughts. Awareness that you are even having thoughts is a good thing! The average person thinks at the "astonishing rate of up to 400 words per minute."[52] The more you are aware of the inane chatter in your head, the more you can distance yourself from it and realize that you are not your thoughts.

But the Law of Attraction has you thinking that you *are* your thoughts. So there I was, with a heightened awareness that I was my thoughts. My thoughts did not like it when my body flew in a plane. I had just come back from a personal vacation on a cruise ship, and the only way to return home as quickly as I wanted or needed was to fly.

On this particular day, I was flying home from San Diego to Victoria. The last section of the flight from Seattle to Victoria was particularly rough. The turbulence literally bounced us into the air a few times. "Empowered" with this new knowledge that I am my thoughts, and that all I have to do is to control my thoughts a little better, I found myself entering a panicked frenzy with the following train of thought:

If I think it, it will come to pass.

Crap. Was that turbulence? Uh oh. It's not stopping. I think this plane will crash.

Damn! I can't think that, cause then the plane will crash.

Stop thinking the plane will crash. Stop thinking the plane will crash. Stop thinking the plane will crash.

I can't stop thinking that the plane will crash.

What if others are thinking that this plane will crash?

Oh my GOD, how many such thoughts are there on the flight today?

Surely this plane will crash. Why is that man praying? What does he know that I don't? Does he have an inside scoop?

Damn! I can't think that because then the plane will crash.

Stop thinking the plane will crash....

and on and on the insanity went.

By this time, I had broken into a damp cold sweat. My heart was pounding, and I felt like it would burst out of my mouth any minute now. And if I kept my mouth shut, it would pop out through my eyes. I had almost stopped breathing. I really felt like I was going to die. It was by far the worst panic attack I have ever experienced. And I don't normally experience panic attacks.

Then, I had an epiphany.

"Wait a doggone minute here," I scolded myself, "it matters not what I think, but what the G—D pilot thinks! I'm not in a position to bring this plane down. He is."

And almost instantaneously, I calmed down. (And, no, the turbulence didn't stop.)

I had this realization, then and there, that you needed to be in a position where you could actively impact the event in order for the event to be realized.

As The Serenity Prayer[53] says:

> *God grant me the serenity*
> *to accept the things I cannot change*
> *courage to change the things I can*
> *and wisdom to know the difference.*

The first fatal flaw of the Law of Attraction (LOA) is that it is not a law. Laws have to be one of two things: they either have to be enforced by an institution (murder is "against the law"), or they have to be an immutable fact ("gravity" cannot be defied here on earth).

The so-called "Law" of Attraction is neither. There are no thought police, and counter to the slick sales pitch, it is not an absolute, unequivocal, unchallenged, undeniable truth. In fact, one of the biggest criticisms about the Law of Attraction is that it is unverifiable.

Many of its proponents call the Law of Attraction an immutable law, and they compare it to the most famous of immutable laws, gravity.[54] That's like comparing apples to clouds.

With the law of gravity, I drop an apple and it falls to the ground. End of demonstration.

With the Law of Attraction, there are no immediate results. In fact, some LOA proponents purport that there is a convenient lag time between the "conceiving" and the "receiving." So if you are inundated with negative thoughts, worry not they tell you; just take our program and we will show you how to manifest. And don't you worry about those negative thoughts you're currently thinking, as the lag time between now and our course is sufficient to offset the damage.

The second fatal flaw is the inferred infallibility of the Law. If you think the *right* thoughts, the right way, with the right emotional intensity and the right fervor, you will see positive results (mostly meaning you will manifest all the money you desire). If you don't see these positive results, it's because you are not managing your thought process appropriately.

Outcomes infer the success of the Law (and again, an immutable law has no measure of success; it can only exist). If Marsha attracted the status of a millionaire, it is because she attracted that into her life by way of maintaining centered thoughts around that goal. And if Veronica failed to attract the status of a millionaire into her life, it is because she inadvertently attracted poverty into her life by way of maintaining centered thoughts around that goal. Marsha is able to stay focused on $1 million; Veronica's thoughts keep on slipping back to poverty.

This inferred infallibility opens the door for the charismatic teacher to make her or his grand entrance and charge what the market will bear. The market will bear what your credit card can carry; after all, what is the meaning of debt when you are learning the guaranteed skills to become undeniably wealthy?

This whole concept plays nicely on human greed. Notice that most law of attraction gurus are focused on helping you become a millionaire, and they weave profound messages of spirituality into their lessons. Very few are focused on establishing something less personally tangible, like world peace. Money is sexy; world peace is a really nice idea, but less lucrative, and available to anyone else who wants to pursue it.

MAPPING THE LAW OF ATTRACTION CONTINUUM

The Law of Attraction is not a singular belief. Like religions and philosophies and musical tastes, we have a spectrum of flavors from which to choose. It ranges from the power of positive thinking to the belief that the universe is entirely of your own making.

Nor is it a singular course. Many (to most) of its teachers focus on wealth acquisition and accumulation, ranging from understanding your money blueprint (T. Harv Eker, Garrett Gunderson) to buying real estate (Robert Allen) to managing investment portfolios (Robert Kiyosaki). Others focus on personal growth (Byron Katie) and spiritual development (Deepak Chopra, Neale Donald Walsch).

The following table is an approximate overview of the personal responsibility assumption made to varying degrees in the Law of Attraction courses currently raging throughout North America and beyond.

I've tried not to pass judgment, as I am convinced that you can learn from just about anyone. While I would not personally take courses from some of the educational forums listed below, I would never go so far as to say they have nothing to offer. Each "teacher" in your life presents you with tools. What you do with them, how you apply them (if you choose to), and what you derive from them, is entirely up to you.

It is included here so that you can see the range. However, it is not definitive. What will make it definitive is your experience (direct or indirect) with it.

	Partial personal responsibility	Substantial personal responsibility	Total personal responsibility
Philosophy	You have some control over the outcomes of your life.	You can shape the outcome of events that impact your life.	You have created every aspect of your life.
Degree of action required	Significant.	Significant. Your thoughts are key, but only if you have the emotional desire to persist through and survive your trials and your failures.	Insignificant. Your thoughts shape everything. That which follows is all a result of your ability to think the right thoughts.
Forums	Books, counseling and therapy sessions, community workshops, one-on-one.	Seminars, classes, leading to larger group.	Seminars, classes, leading to larger group.
Examples	Positive-thought proponents, authors, counselors, Alcoholics Anonymous. Dale Carnegie's How to Win Friends and Influence People 1. Fundamental Techniques in Handling People 2. Six Ways to Make People Like You 3. Twelve Ways to Win People to Your Way of Thinking 4. Be a Leader: How to Change People Without Giving Offense or Arousing Resentment 5. Letters That Produced Miraculous Results 6. Eight Rules For Making your Home Life Happier	Events happen to you; how you respond to those events will have a significant ability to shape your future. Jack Canfield's formula E+R = O encapsulates it (Events + Response = Outcome). Napoleon Hill advocated that you can receive what you conceive if you have an intense burning desire driving your action.	Landmark Education. Their philosophy is that personal responsibility begins and ends with one's willingness to be central cause of all results in one's life. Being both the cause and the effect is the ideal way to to live. T. Harv Eker's T F A R formula encapsulates it (Thoughts lead to Feelings lead to Action lead to Results). It's all you.

	Partial personal responsibility	Substantial personal responsibility	Total personal responsibility
Extreme examples		Your negative thoughts contributed toward your current situation. If you are down, it's because you don't believe you are worth better.	Pat Robertson, an evangelical Christian suggests that the recent Haiti earthquake was brought about by the Haitians themselves in a deal they made with the devil to free them from the French.
Further research	Irrelevant to the success of the relationship.	Encouraged. The greater your exposure, the greater your chances at success.	Not encouraged. The knowledge you will receive here is definitive. Stay away from the negative influence of fear-mongering newspapers and magazines.
Costs might fall into this range	$20/book Free consultation then typically $30-$50-$100/session depending on the type	Free intro nights $100-1000/classes $50-$500+/session	Free intro nights $500-$30,000+/ seminars Seminars are frequently hosted by a high-profile success story, and run behind the scenes by volunteers.
Types	Positive thinking Therapy Counseling Community classes	Community classes Seminars	Seminars Several of the Large Group Awareness Training (LGAT) programs
Techniques	Comfort zone is challenged Guided learning Journaling Peer-led group study	Comfort zone is challenged Mental breakdowns lead to breakthroughs Call-and-response technique	Comfort zone is challenged Mental breakdowns lead to breakthroughs Deprivation (contact, food/beverage, bathrooms, etc.)

	Partial personal responsibility	Substantial personal responsibility	Total personal responsibility
Techniques Cont'd.			Group chants or call-and-response technique
			Deviation from the group can lead to personal humiliation
			Independent thinking is discouraged (you are here, after all, because you are a failure and you want to learn from the successful expert so shut up and learn)
Spirituality	Not typically present unless specifically seeking religious or spiritual guidance	Implicit or explicit religious overtones	Implicit or explicit religious overtones
Qualifications/ Status	Academic achievement	Track record success	Cult-like status of the guru
			Group conversations discouraged
			Challenging the teachings discouraged (you can be physically removed from the session)
The Interpretation of Failure	Failure means you haven't yet been able to turn it around and look at it from a different perspective.	Failure means you are one step closer to success. Success is built on a succession of failures.	Failure means you are personally being punished. You haven't "played" at 120%. You are personally weak. Typically, more classes will help you achieve a better rate of success.
The Interpretation of Success	You can live in your current circumstances and be a happier human being.	You can persist through the rough times knowing that the plan and the journey will get you there.	You will be rich.

The Law of Attraction, wrapped in its mantra of self-improvement in the names of God and Wealth, makes for a lucrative industry. In 2006, the research firm Marketdata estimated the "self-improvement" business in the U.S. generated more than $9 billion in sales—including infomercials, mail-order catalogs, holistic institutes, books, audio cassettes, motivation-speaker seminars, the personal coaching market, weight-loss and stress-management programs.[55] It's also an unregulated field, which means it's buyer beware.

SPOTTING THE SLICK SNAKE-OIL SALESMAN

I include here an interview that Michael Lovitch (owner of The Hypnosis Network in Dallas Texas) had with Dave Lakhani[56] (a marketing expert and persuasion specialist, NLP practitioner, speaker, author, and trainer). The interview took place in the aftermath of three deaths in a sweat lodge on October 8, 2009, at a self-improvement event in Sedona, Arizona.[57]

Lovitch and Lakhani speak about "cult awareness, guru protection, or how to think independently." Lakhani details how coercive groups tempt you to part with your money in return for insider information. The following is a direct transcript of Lakhani's information.

1. You start out by pointing to people's shortcomings their missed hopes and dreams and when possible you point them to existing large beliefs sets around religion or philosophical constructs that appear to support the behavior that they hope to learn as being the cause of their missed hopes and dreams.

2. Then you suggest there is knowledge that exists that always existed that's available if you know how to access it.

3. Then you position a charismatic talking head as the leader and dispenser of the secrets.

4. You demonstrate how the leader has persevered and learned the secrets and is now willing to reveal them to you, you are so fortunate.

5. You tie the knowledge to mystical practices, to ancient civilizations or societies, and to supposed laws or mystical places.

6. You make very tenuous ties using social proof backed science particularly science most people don't understand like quantum physics.

7. You make acceptance of the secret exclusive often based on price.

8. You encourage people to act alike, dress alike, pray together, and take aggressively more aggressive behaviors together. You have them shave their heads, fast, engage in exhaustive prayer, deprive them of sleep, food, contact with others.

9. Use noise and light discipline. Practice sensory overload and deprivation.

10. Discourage logical thinking and reward faith.

11. Encourage them by telling them pushing past the boundaries is part of their initiation into a new way of being.

12. You have them value being misunderstood by their peers and have them use that lack of understanding by their peers as validation that they are in fact moving in the right direction.

13. You offer them progressively more esoteric opportunities for more money of course with no real quantifiable measurable results.

14. You give the group names, rites of passage, special ways of knowing or recognizing each other.

15. You forbid them from sharing the secret knowledge or events that occurred during their initiation with others so that those people, should they become enlightened enough as well, are not deprived of the opportunity to fully experience what's happening.

16. And then when things go wrong you bring it back to the leaders pain and rally the true believers around him, get them to talk about how terrible the leader feels and have them express what his internal condition is. Make it about his suffering and not that of the effected.

17. You turned the attention to the teachings and the teacher not the failure.

Lifelong learning is critical to growth. It is critical that you seek the right teachers, the teachers who best speak to you, who can best complement your objectives, and who work in your best interests. The world is also full of "snake oil" sellers, those interested in selling you "secret" solutions with questionable or unverifiable results.

All forms of education matter. Learning is important. Anyone who augments your growth and spurs you forward has served a greater purpose. Spend your money wisely. When considering any self-improvement courses, ask someone who has previously taken the course. Don't ask people whether they enjoyed the course, or whether it generated enthusiasm. Ask how the course has impacted their business or career or passions.

If you believe that the Law of Attraction will carry you through from beginning to end without any additional effort on your part other than sustaining a thought, then you can put down this book right now. Keep on thinking your thoughts and manifesting your future.

If you would like to augment your thoughts and beliefs with initiative and action, then the remaining chapters are for you.

Chapter 9

CHANGING YOUR MIND(SET)

OPENING YOUR MIND TO POSITIVE POSSIBILITY

Change is inevitable. The seasons change. You grow older. Your darling obedient children become beastly rebellious teenagers (speaking from experience here!). You get fired or hired. You experience the death of a loved one; you experience the birth of a new-to-be loved one. There's a pulse to nature that you cannot separate yourself from, try as you may. The universal spirit of change craves continuously to express itself.

This longing and natural inclination for growth is repressed in many of us because of negative thinking and unconstructive programming based in our past experiences and anticipated fears. A lack of trust in our own abilities and natural talents hinders us dramatically.

Each of us has a dual nature. One part wants to move forward and embrace change; the other wants to pull back and keep things the same. What you focus on expands. The part that you cultivate determines your final results in life. Both parts will seek to dominate, but you control which side wins.

Those who cannot change their minds cannot change anything.
— George Bernard Shaw

People often believe their own experience is a universal truth. "Because I see this tree from this view, it is all there is." Others accept their own experience as something that happened and realize there are many truths. "Because I see this tree from this view, it is what I see, and there are other places to stand, other ways to experience this tree"—from the ground, from a plane, from the moon, from under the earth, from inside the tree; or, as a seedling, a shade provider, a piece of lumber, a chair, or firewood.

Become the Open Mind and Acquire a Mindset Open to Possibility

The person with an open mind does not just gather information. She considers the possibilities and other interpretations before reaching any conclusion.

When she closes her mind, she tells her higher self, including the "powers of the universe," that she cannot grow and thereby cuts off any hope of progressive transformation. The closed mind gathers dust!

What your conscious mind sees, believes, feels, and thinks is conveyed to the subconscious mind; your subconscious mind determines how you will react when opportunities present themselves.

Examples of Negative Thinking

You may have heard that the brain can't process negative thoughts. I think this statement is both true and untrue.

A favorite example used by Neurolinguistic Programming practitioners is The Pink Elephant. They suggest that our brain does not receive information presented in the negative, and in part, I believe they are correct. If I say to you, "Do NOT think of a pink elephant with purple polka dots on her big floppy ears and a trunk painted red," you will find yourself thinking precisely of the image I described, in all its detail.

Optimism is the faith that leads to achievement. Nothing can be done without hope or confidence.
— Helen Keller

Likewise, if you tell a child "not to fall," you draw her attention specifically to the possibility of falling. It may be better to focus on what you do want (a positive command) and say, "Watch your balance."

The brain cannot process in the negative when that negative is stated as a visual. Don't think of a pink elephant, and sure enough you're thinking of that pink elephant. At the same time, we are extraordinarily skilled at focusing on the negative, or on the traits that we feel we lack, every time we doubt our own abilities. For example, if your inner critic says, "You can't draw worth a lick, and you're not funny, so don't bother dreaming that you can be a cartoonist," your brain does NOT delete the negative and convert it into the positive: "I can draw and am funny and will be a cartoonist." Instead, you agonize over it, bemoan your lack of talent, and quit altogether.

The difference lies in the context. With the explicit command, "Don't think of a pink elephant," you actually have to consider the object (the pink elephant) in order to understand the sentence. It is an unemotional static event, externally issued.

Internally issued events have a different set of rules, especially those that have strong emotions attached to them. Consider chronic, life-long habits and beliefs, those where you've continually told yourself that "I can't win; there's no hope; I'm a loser." These do in fact reinforce a negative belief.

A constellation of internally issued, emotionally-based beliefs (I'm a loser; there's no hope; I can't win) is different from a single, unemotional command, "Don't think of a pink elephant" that has been externally issued.

In this way, we are capable of thinking in the negative.

Examples of Positive Thinking

I'm sure you've heard of the "half-empty" proverb: Is the glass half-empty or half-full?

My grandmother, my dear sad Oma, recently suffered a stroke. The term *stroke* conjures up images of life-long debilitation.

Oma was taken to the hospital and spent three days in the hallways while the staff tried to find a room for her. On the first day, she couldn't speak. She is prone to dramatic storytelling, and being unable to articulate her suffering caused her great distress. By the second day, she could speak again and was wandering through the halls to check in on the other patients. By the third day, she was talking up a storm.

Oma fully recovered from a stroke after only three days. The doctors kept her for two more days for observation and then sent her home, where she continues to live independently.

Were her "glass of life" half-full, she'd surely look at her experience and count her blessings. Not many eighty-five-year-olds get off so easily after having a stroke! Many are wheelchair-bound for the rest of their lives, some are locked in their own bodies, having lost the capacity to communicate, and others have compound speech and muscular issues.[57]

Yet my Oma was up and running within two weeks, fit as a weasel. You'd never look at her and see any signs of a stroke.

Unfortunately, my negative-bound Oma is committed to reliving only misery. She remembers only the inconsistent care at the hospital, the roughness of one nurse, the panic of not being able to speak, the fear of permanent aphasia.

She spirals with these thoughts clutched tightly against her heart into the possibility of future pain.

If your glass is "half-empty," you focus on what's gone (and may never re-appear) and you desperately cling to what is left. The scarcity mentality sets in. "I can never consume this because LOOK WHAT HAPPENS. It disappears, and I have to hang on to what is left. My life depends on it!" In Oma's case, life now begins and ends with her miserable hospital experience. A minor headache turns into weeping and then into heaving, full-body sobs. Any mention of the hospital takes her back to her state of misery.

When your glass is half-empty, you mourn what is gone; when your glass is half-full, you focus on the wealth or the abundance of any situation. Balance comes from acknowledging the empty and savoring the remaining parts. You recognize what was, appreciate what is, and anticipate what will be. And perhaps, that the glass can always be refilled.

You can spiral into the positive by focusing on the following:

- Availability instead of scarcity.
- Joy instead of sorrow.
- Anticipation instead of fear.

Whether you approach your life as half-empty or half-full makes all the difference. *What you carry with you into the present is what your future will bring.*

The Optimist and the Pessimist

A family had twin girls whose only resemblance to each other was their looks. If one said a movie was too loud, the other said it was too quiet. If one wanted her hair curled, the other wanted hers straightened. If one wanted to wear a dress, the other would wear pants. If one felt it was too hot, the other thought it was too cold. One was an eternal optimist, the other a doom-and-gloom pessimist.

They were opposite in absolutely every way imaginable.

The twins' tenth birthday arrived. Curious to see what might happen, their mother loaded the pessimist's room with every imaginable toy and game. There were dolls, crafts and puzzles, new clothes, hair accessories and footwear—everything a girl could want. Then, the mother loaded the optimistic sister's room with one single item: she filled the floor with horse manure.

After the girls came home from school, the one dashed and the other one sauntered into her respective room to see what gifts had befallen her on this golden day. A few minutes later, the mother passed by the pessimist's room. She found her sitting amid her new gifts, crying bitterly.

"Why are you crying?" the mother asked.

"Because these aren't the presents I wanted. Some need to have batteries. Others I know I'll get bored with really soon. And none of my friends have boots like these; they have the ones with the thick high heels, not low ones," answered the doom-and-gloom twin. The mother left this twin to her misery.

Then heading into the optimist twin's room, the mother found her singing for joy while shoveling the manure out of the window. "What are you so happy about?" the mother asked.

The optimistic twin replied, "Well, with all of this horse poop in my room, there's got to be a pony in the house somewhere!"[58]

While this story is a little contrived and incredibly unlikely, it does make the point that optimism (or pessimism) is contained not in the actual event itself, but in the understanding and the interpretation of the event.

THE FOUR STAGES OF LEARNING

When I teach my Confidence 101 workshops, I discuss the four stages of learning.

The first stage of the learning curve is being unconsciously unskilled. In other words, you don't know what you don't know.

Consider a newborn baby. A baby is born with absolutely no knowledge of the value of her four flailing appendages beyond the fact that they periodically thwack her in the face and cause momentary discomfort. That baby does not know what she doesn't know, and consequently, those appendages have no significant value.

You know you're in the first stage, unconscious incompetence, when:

- You believe you know everything you need to know.
- You're confident and comfortable with what is.
- New information is not welcomed or required.

When a child begins to grasp for things, begins to crawl, and begins to walk, she learns that those appendages have purpose. She notices how others use their appendages to eat, acquire things, and move about. She has entered into the second stage of learning: she has become conscious of what she doesn't know. This is conscious incompetence.

In the second stage, people usually quit unless their motivation—the why—is big enough to see them through the potential failures. The child does not quit because for her, the goal of learning to walk is non-negotiable. She will try and fail until she masters her task no matter what.

You know you're in the second stage when:

- You become aware that there is something else.
- You see others applying some skill that you have not yet acquired.
- You want to acquire that skill.

When the child begins to walk, she is not very good at it. She falls down. She gets up. She falls down. She gets up again. She falls down and hits her head on the corner of the coffee table. She cries. She gets up again. Each time she gets up, she has improved.

In the third stage of learning, you are consciously applying the skills you have learned. Your brain is pretty full applying this new knowledge; in fact, your brain may be so full that things you easily were able to do previously are now all but lost and forgotten; all your brain power is now dedicated to this particular task.

You know you're in the third stage, conscious competence, when:

- You are applying a new skill.
- You're not very good at it.
- You've forgotten other things you once knew.
- You fail a lot.
- You feel like giving up.

The final state of learning is when you become unconsciously competent. Most of us have become unconsciously competent walkers. When we walk, we don't need to scan the ground for obstacles. We are able to engage our peripheral vision to forewarn our bodies of uncovered service holes, dog poop, and stones. Have you ever seen a four-year-old child nearly walk off a sidewalk curb because she was single-mindedly focused on the doll in her hands? For a four-year-old, walking is still risky business, but not so much for the forty-year-old! By that age, we have mastered the skill.

You know you're in the fourth stage, unconscious competence, when:

- You believe you know everything you need to know.
- You are confident and comfortable with what is.
- New information is not welcomed or required.

Sound familiar?

THE CONFIDENCE CURVE

The confidence curve nestles nicely against the four stages of learning as represented in the following diagram:

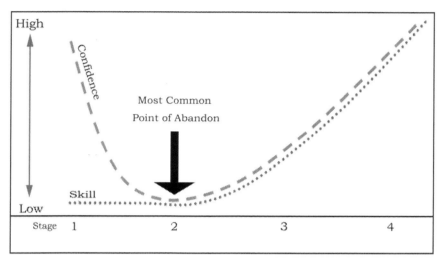

When you first approach a new skill, your competence in that new skill is low, and because you don't yet know what you don't know, your confidence may be high.

Have you ever watched a baseball game on TV? I'm a bit of a couch sports surfer, and baseball as a sport amuses me (to boredom, hence these analogies). However, were I to step beyond the couch sports-surfing mode and begin to learn what it would take for me to become a league player, I would have to begin learning what it is that I don't know.

Did you know that there are specific techniques to batting the ball? Prior to writing this section, I thought it was as simples as connecting the bat with the ball. I didn't know what I didn't know. Then, I after accepting that perhaps it was more complicated than that, I set out to research (learn) what I didn't know. Upon entering the second phase, I learned that the needed skills would include the following:

- Selecting the right bat.

- Holding the bat properly (knuckles lined up, with a loose grip, and knowing when to load, especially with the top hand).

- Assuming the proper batter's box stance (standing in the middle or standing deep in the box, with an open, even, or closed stance—which is best determined by the flexibility and rotating the hips).

- Knowing how to read the pitcher.

- Anticipating the point of contact.

- Knowing the strike zone.

- Being aggressive with every pitch, knowing how to "load and stride" so as to be ready to explode into a hit at any time.

- Knowing when to swing and understanding the location of the bat's "sweet spot" (two to six inches from the end of the bat, depending of course on the bat).

- Knowing properly how to follow through once contact with the ball has been made (the barrel of the bat should wrap around the upper back).

- Knowing when not to swing.

- Being fearless.[59]

Typically, when you enter Stage 2 and begin learning how much you really don't know, your confidence plummets. Can you imagine if someone called me up and placed me in the middle of practice session with the New York Yankees? My confidence would drop to the floor.

Should I dedicate myself to the sport for many years and really learn it (Stage 3), my confidence would increase with each new milestone. Maybe I wouldn't strike out but get walked to first base, and then maybe I would foul a ball, and then I would hit a ball halfway back to the pitcher.

Were I to master the skills needed for a major league baseball player (become unconsciously competent), I might even one day be invited to play on my local town's team; at that point, my confidence would soar.

In our undertakings, we typically begin with high confidence. This confidence gives us enough momentum to move to (and through) the second stage, where confidence plummets as we discover how little we actually know. It takes a strong (accountable) person to recognize personal room for growth, to recognize one's own imperfections. As our skills grow (and with the proper collaborative groups in place), our confidence increases until we can apply the new learning without thinking about it. Once again, we are at the peak of our confidence.

Many experts say that Stage 1 is the best place to begin a new learning venture. Your confidence is at its highest, and your skill set is at its lowest, although you don't know it and are not going to inundate yourself with negative self-talk. With enough momentum to propel you through Stage 2, you can arrive at Stage 3 and proceed to Stage 4. Arrogance and ignorance, followed by sheer determination and stubborn persistence, and accompanied by accountability and collaborative supports, is a great formula for success.

CALL TO ACTION

Where are you right now within your comfort zone, and how does this align with the confidence curve?

1. What skills are you using in your business and personal life that require little or no thinking? In what areas are you unconsciously competent?

2. In what areas are you consciously incompetent? What skills do you know that you need to brush up on?

3. When learning a new skill, how do you typically respond to failure?

> *A person who never made a mistake never tried anything new.*
> — Albert Einstein

GETTING OUT OF YOUR COMFORT ZONE

It is easy to live your entire life seeking only comfort and easy answers and avoiding challenge, but doing so means never growing. It is not living, but merely existing. To live perpetually in your comfort zone is to live perpetually in the unconscious.

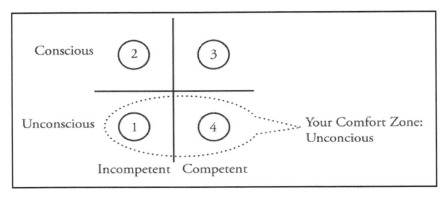

Anthony Robbins has another way of charting it by describing four classes of experience.

- **Class 1:** Peak life experiences. Life is and feels good for you and others, and it serves the greater good. Class 1 is the class we are always striving to achieve. It is equivalent to being in the comfort zone in a positive and perfect way.

- **Class 2:** Brings the most pleasure. Its experiences bring you the most triumphs, the most joy, but they are also the most avoided. They are good for you and others, and they serve the greater good, but it's hell to step out of this comfort zone and grow. Have you ever worked hard for something? Something you knew you could achieve but had to work hard for, against the odds? I'll bet you felt exhilarated once you crossed the finish line. Class 1 *sounds like* the ultimate place to be, but Class 2 is actually the most rewarding. **Productively stepping out of the comfort zone really occurs only in Class 2.**

> Life is either a daring adventure or nothing at all. Security is mostly a superstition. It does not exist in nature.
> — Helen Keller

- **Class 3:** Immediately gratifying. Experiences that feel good but are actually bad for you and others and don't serve the greater good. Bad habits such as excessive alcohol consumption or smoking cigarettes fall into this category. This can be thought of as a comfort zone in the negative. You know you need to stop smoking, and you know smoking can take decades off your life, but you've smoked for so long that quitting probably won't make a great deal of a difference. You think, "I'll smoke for now and put off the quitting for another day. Maybe it'll be next year's resolution. Again."

- **Class 4:** Bad all around. Experiences that feel and are bad for you and for others and do not serve the greater good. These activities are typically done under peer pressure; everyone else is doing it. It is also a negative comfort zone. Behaviors could include staying in an abusive relationship because of coercion and your own fear.

The chart of these classes of experience looks like this.

		How it is for you	How it is for others	How it serves the greater good	How it feels for you
Good		Class 1	Class 1	Class 1	Class 1
		Class 2	Class 2	Class 2	Class 3
Bad		Class 3	Class 3	Class 3	Class 2
		Class 4	Class 4	Class 4	Class 4

Class 2 is the only class that benefits you, that serves you in the long run, and that requires you to step out of your comfort zone and grow.

In his book *Finding Serenity in the Age of Anxiety*, Robert Gerzon explores the idea of the comfort zone. He writes that the "comfort zone's physiological basis lies in our body's need to maintain *homeostasis*, a certain range of conditions that allow for optimal functioning." In other words, we learn throughout our lives how to moderate our behavior so we comply with family and societal norms. The secret of the comfort zone is that the more wisely we challenge it, the better it functions. "Having a comfort zone is healthy; being imprisoned in one is not".[61]

Gerzon identifies two "walls" that keep us locked in our comfort zone: The Wall of Anxiety (hyperactivity; doing without results) and The Wall of Depression (lethargy; not doing without becoming rested).[62] He presents what he calls "The Comfort Zone Cycle," in which we find ourselves stuck between extreme hyperactivity (frenzied activity at work) and extreme lethargy (turning on the TV and "vegging out" after dinner).[63] One extreme begets the physiological need for the other to kick in. Like a perpetual pendulum, we swing back and forth *inside* the comfort zone without ever achieving either serenity or an actual goal.

Our frenzied work life keeps us swearing we'll leave our job before it kills us, but we go home and "veg" as the reward or justification for a hard day's work. After we've vegged too much, we berate ourselves for wasting away hours and not writing that book we've always wanted to write, not going to the gym, not meditating, or whatever we choose for raking ourselves over the coals. We continually ricochet between depression and anxiety.

We may set goals that are within the preexisting comfort zone. From the outside view, it will look like we are doing something productive. On the inside, however, we continue this crazy ricocheting until a crisis hits and we are forced out of our comfort zones. We get fired or divorced. A loved one dies. Often, it is these life-altering events that shake us out of our comfort zone and challenge us to go for more.

More effective ways than undergoing stressful life-altering events, however, can be found to break through the walls of depression and toxic anxieties. The initial work is done by focusing on the space between your ears. Gerzon offers his A+ formula:

- **Awareness**. Know that you may not know all the answers. Know that you may need to learn. Know that you may need to step out of your comfort zone. As Einstein says, changing your current level of awareness is the only way to solve any problem effectively.

- **Acceptance**. Accept the situation as it is, in this very moment. If you're being laid off, then you need to move from this point forward. Thinking you will lose your home and get divorced as a result of this layoff is a form of Toxic Anxiety. Accept that you are now jobless and have a problem to solve.

- **Analysis**. Analyze that problem. See what you can do about it; see the myriad of solutions and opportunities available to you.

- **Action**. Take an action, immediately. Do something. Write a plan. Call someone. Sign up for a course. Anything. If doesn't matter whether you are met with failure or adversity. The "win" comes from taking action.

- **Appreciation**. When all is said and done, appreciate life for the experiences it has given you. Remember that each obstacle is a blessing in disguise.

The first step, as Gerzon suggest in this list, is awareness. Start to realize that the bulk of your day—by virtue of being human—is spent in your comfort zone. Increasing your awareness will also build your ability to see solutions, for it's not until you recognize rote behavior that you can do anything about it.

You may have heard it suggested that you begin stepping out of your comfort zone by taking a different way to work in the morning. For some, that might work. I'm suggesting something more subtle: Instead of taking a new way to work every morning, start noticing different things on your way to work.

Have you ever walked by a major demolition site in an area that you pass by regularly and wondered what it was that was torn down? I was recently met by a gaping hole in the middle of Victoria in an area close to where I used to live, and I could not remember what it was that stood there prior. Was it a business building? An apartment block? A parking lot? I honestly had no idea.

It is not just the little things that we fail to notice. It's also the big things. It is said that a fish doesn't notice the water in which it swims. Likewise, we humans tend not to notice the everyday things in our environments, in our lives, small or big.

Becoming aware of your habitual behavior, your habitual way of responding to challenges and changes, to success and to failures is the first step you can take to stepping out of your comfort zone.

Once you've noticed it, then you can step beyond it.

In the text that follows, right through to the end of the book, we are going to look at some tools that will help you break down the barriers that keep you locked inside your comfort zone.

THE THREE MOST DANGEROUS WORDS

I started teaching a course on confidence in 2008. This course always begins with this question:

"What are the three most dangerous words in the English language?"

Students will typically come up with a standard list of negatives, such as "No can do," or "That is impossible," or "That's too hard," or "I can't do that."

> *The first problem for all of us, men and women, is not to learn, but to unlearn.*
> — Gloria Steinem

After they run out of sentences, I turn to the flip chart and write, in big block letters:

"I KNOW THAT!"

In the moment when you *think* you know everything, all learning potential has grounded to a dead stop.

You may have heard of the allegory of The Cave, as described by Socrates.

Imagine a cave inhabited by a captivated population that has been immobilized since birth by chains. In addition to their bound torsos, arms, and legs, their heads are also fixed: they are compelled to gaze only at the wall in front of them.

Shadows appear on this wall, as the people and animals beyond the cave move by. Their noises echo inside the cave.

The people captivated in the cave know only these shadows. Socrates argued that the cave dwellers would establish an understanding of the world based only on these shadows. This understanding would establish their rules, their laws of functioning.

Socrates then speculated about what might happen if one person broke free from the chains and stumbled out of the cave. Coming from the darkness into the light, the person would be initially (and temporarily) blinded. Once that person's eyes adjusted, the living forms would be unrecognizable. Translating two dimensions (shadows) into three (form) would make a direct understanding impossible.

The person's instinct would be to return to the cave where all shapes were known and understood, neatly defined and categorized.

However, as the "liberated" person spent time outside the cave, the person would adjust and ultimately accept this new perspective as normal.[65]

Once this person has entered into a new reality, a new perspective, a return to the old new way of thinking becomes unthinkable. Returning to the cave is not an option. Do you remember the words of Morpheus in the movie *The Matrix*? *"You take the blue pill, the story ends—you wake up in your bed and believe whatever you want to believe. You take the red pill, you stay in Wonderland, and I show you how deep the rabbit hole goes."*

Whatever your current view is, whatever cave you're in, there is *always* another way of experiencing life. That viewpoint may be completely opposite to yours *and* completely "correct" at the same time.

The movie *What the Bleep Do We Know!?: Down the Rabbit Hole*—a lively introduction to metaphysical thought—throws the following statistics at the viewer:

- The average human being receives 400 billion bits of information per second.

- The average human being is aware of 2,000 bits of information per second.

- The average human being has one thought per second and a guesstimated 60,000 thoughts per day—most of which are executed on autopilot.

Here's an easy way to consider these figures: When you watch a television show, you are focused on what's happening with the main characters, but a great deal of activity is taking place in the background:

- Frequent lens changes and perspective changes
- Time shifts

- Background music
- Commercials
- Whatever is happening in your living space
- Telephone calls
- Children playing
- Someone speaking in the background
- The ticking of a clock
- Outside road and air traffic
- The housefly

Equally important are the things that exist for the actor(s) but are completely and entirely hidden from your view: the cameras, the director, the writers, the continuity person, the casting director and so on.

If your conscious brain had to stop to notice and absorb each bit of information it received, if your conscious brain had to be aware of the process of creation, an act as simple as watching a movie would be impossible.

This is both the blessing and the curse of focus. Focus lets us "know" things; it lets us experience, learn, and grow, but it also tricks us into thinking that our knowledge is definitive.

Whenever you find yourself uttering those dangerous words, "I know that," stop and reconsider. You know only your worldview, and there may be (in fact, there are) others.

To paraphrase Einstein, when you accept that you don't know, you change your level of awareness, and by doing so, by embracing new possibilities, you can stop repeating the same unworkable "fixes" to the same problems.

THE POWER OF BECOMING: LEARNING TO EXIST AS IF

One fellow I coached—I'll call him Lucky—recently underwent a nasty custody battle for his one son. Lucky's family and friends wanted to protect him, and they tried to prepare him for his eventual loss. Women always win the custody battles, he was told, because the courts favor the mothers. His first lawyer shared this view. In addition to the venomous relationship he had with his ex-wife, Lucky developed an intense anger against the system that seemed to be working against him by virtue of his anatomy.

Having studied the field of productive and positive thinking, and having counseled other clients navigating emotional abysses, I had some different advice for him.

"Are you willing to accept the outcome that your ex will have primary custody of your son?" I asked him.

"F—k no!" was his venomous reply.

"Then you need to change your question," I said.

"What do you mean?" he asked.

"Instead of asking yourself IF you will get primary custody, ask yourself WHEN. Banish all thoughts of any other outcome. Act as if it is inevitable that you will be assigned primary custody of your son, and the only unknown you have to contend with is when, and that you won't stop until you have accomplished this."[65]

The custody battle took the better part of two years. These were by far the most difficult two years of his life. But in the end, he won primary custody of his son.

> To be a great champion you must believe you are the best. If you're not, pretend you are.
> — Muhammad Ali

Changing the question from *if* to *when* allowed Lucky to build a team of people who would help him achieve the only outcome he was willing to accept. He ditched his initial lawyer and found an incredibly smart and compassionate female lawyer. Between my advice and his lawyer's brilliance (mostly the latter!), Lucky found the strength to keep his focus on the end result, and he managed to keep his fears and doubts at bay.

I have had my own experience of existing "as if" many times.

When I stood for the first time in front of a class of new motorcycle riders looking to learn from an experienced instructor, I had to present myself "as if" I truly knew what I was doing. I had about a year's worth of training under my belt along with eight years of riding accident-free, but I'd never actually taught before.

When I first visited my older brother at the University of Guelph, I was a high school dropout working for pennies at Chicken Express. Standing on the campus, I knew I was breathing the air of my own future. Graduating from college became, in that instant, my "as if." Everything I did that followed moved me closer to my goal of stepping foot on a campus of my own, which I did a few years later.

And when I set out to ride my motorcycle from St. John's Newfoundland to Victoria, BC to start a new life, no alternative outcome came to my mind. I had already arrived in my mind. It was now not a question of *if* but *when*, and I would enjoy the journey.

EMPLOYING SELF-TALK TO SHAPE YOUR SELF

Why do you think business and strategic plans are so incredibly important?

Why do you think many coaches and counselors recommend you keep a journal?

Why do you think English teachers make you write book reports?

The answers are all the same: Not because they'll collect dust for three years as they sit on the shelf and slowly disintegrate. Not because of the pretty front covers. Not because of your penmanship or the font you choose. Not because of your skill of structuring paragraphs and sentences. But rather, because the *process* of writing lets you turn the abstract concept known as a thought or opinion into a concretely worded articulate analysis, perhaps even with an actionable plan.

Consider the power of the word in another concept. Have you ever had an incredibly great day, where you just *knew* you looked great in those clothes you were wearing, you just *knew* your hair shone and your ruddy face exuded utter brilliance and happiness. You just *knew* things were going to go right for you that day.

And then…Margaret from Accounting comes up to you and says, "Oh dear [insert your name here], what's wrong? You look incredibly tired. Have you gained weight?"

And BAMMM! There you are, wearing your self-esteem around your ankles for the rest of the day or perhaps even week.

Margaret's thoughts aren't what brought you down. It wasn't her vibrational energy or intent. Had she kept her mouth shut and her words neatly tucked inside, you wouldn't have cared in the least. Instead, she released those words. And those words created a new reality of you, one you didn't see, let alone anticipate.

Or perhaps you have done that to someone else? I remember once when I was about seven or eight, gaily singing Christmas songs at the top of my lungs when my older brother Tom turned to me and spat out the words, "Shuddap. You can't sing." His words created my reality for the next twenty years. He may not even remember the event. He was after all, my older brother who wanted nothing more than not to listen to his bratty little sister bellow. His intentions were to "dis" me in the moment. And then, he let it go. But I hung onto his words for an awfully long time, and sentenced myself to mouthing silently the words to "Happy Birthday to You" forever after at birthday parties.

What kind of creating are *you* doing with your own words, with your own self-talk, with your own *thoughts?*

Have you ever considered the language that you use, your word choice, and how it shapes who you are? Does your language tend to be passive and overly forgiving when you talk to others?

- Passive ("Someone needs to help out with this.")

- Negative ("You probably already know this but...")

- Omissions ("What would you like to do tonight?")

- Insufficient insistence ("What do you think of...")

- Retraction (use of minimizing words like "perhaps," "maybe," "what if")

- Intentionally undermined intelligence (catering to the intelligence of others in order to come across as agreeable; "Of course!" when you secretly add "not" under your breath; "How true" when it's dead wrong; "Yep" when you really mean "Nope. What are you, an idiot?")

What about when you talk to yourself? What exactly are you saying? Are you speaking the truth in kindness? Are you open to possibility? Or do you shut yourself down with internal chatter that breeds doubt, worry, and fear?

CALL TO ACTION

I learned this exercise during my counseling days. Take a blank piece of paper and divide it into two parts, with a line down the middle.

One the left side, record your negative self-talk.

On the right, dispute the negativity, and rework it with a more positive tone or outcome.

Negative Self-Talk	Dispute and Rework It
Oh my GOD, I've just been fired. I'm going to lose my shirt, my house, and my husband. How am I ever going to get through this living hell?	Oh my GOD Auntie May! How did you get into my head?! Of course I'm scared. I'm scared because I don't know what tomorrow will bring. But I've been scared before. Like the time when I was eleven and got lost in the Amsterdam airport. Or the time we had the house fire. Or the time I got divorced. I survived those, and I can survive these. Thanks for caring, Auntie May, but I don't need your fears at this time. I've got work to do! Options to explore! Maybe now I can start that business I always wanted. Thanks for sharing, but buh-bye Auntie!

Now you can try reworking some of your negative self-talk. Have fun with it!

Negative Self-Talk	Dispute and Rework It

You can also turn your language "up a notch." Have you ever gone into the grocery store and had a robotic cashier say to you (without even looking at you), "How's your day?" Like most other people, you probably reply just as mechanically, "Okay, thanks."

I always turn it up a notch. I say with great exuberance, "Fantastic!!! Thanks so much for asking. And yours?" When a customer says something delightfully unexpected, like "Fantastic!" the cashier will stop and take notice.

Instead of saying		Say	
I feel	good	I feel	fantastic
	okay		awesome
	motivated		driven
	confident		unstoppable

Your vocabulary impacts how you feel.

1. Write down some of the positive (or extremely positive) words you have used in the past.

2. Write down some of your old good phrases.

3. Replace your old phrases with phrases using magnificent words and magnificent phrases.

WHEN TO SAY "I'M SORRY"

Two groups of people are renowned for their craving to apologize: Canadians and women. (I am Canadian *and* a woman and therefore know of what I write!) Do you belong to one of these two groups? Do you tend to apologize for everything? Do you find yourself apologizing for:

- Being late

- Being early

- Being on time when the other person is late or early

- Being stepped on

- Bumping into someone

- Someone bumping into you

- Asserting yourself into a conversation

- Insisting on being heard

Start paying attention to your apologies. Over-apologizing makes our apologies useless and insincere. To have currency, to hold value, an apology has to be real.

Fake apologies are just as damaging to the spirit. Here are some examples:

- "I'm sorry I didn't call—I've been really busy." (Crudely translated: Please be understanding about the fact that other things were more important than you.)

- "I'm sorry you feel that way. It wasn't what I meant." (Crudely translated: I think it's too bad that you had difficulty understanding me correctly.)

- "I'm sorry if I offended you…" (Crudely translated: I can't think of anything I did wrong, but if you think so, I'd be happy to apologize so I can get back in your good graces.)

If you are going to apologize, do it intentionally and with meaning. Identify the situations in which you give automatic or insincere apologies, and STOP faking it!

Only say "I'm sorry" when you mean it and can specify exactly for what you are apologizing.

When we give what I believe is a healthy or authentic apology, we can state clearly what we did that was disrespectful or inconsiderate without:

- explaining why we did it.
- telling someone that he or she misunderstood our real intention.
- bringing up some other issue that suggests that the other person contributed to or caused the problem.

If we can change how we give and receive apologies, we can become less defensive, gain insight, and wisdom, and strengthen all of our relationships. We can also be a strong model for others, teaching them that real apologies show strength of character and foster respect.

STEPPING INTO YOUR ASPIRATIONS

Body Language

Remember the scene I presented earlier—a woman walking through a parking lot late at night? In one scenario, her body language was silent and scared; in the other, it was strong and bold.

What you choose to assert through body language is often done unconsciously and may be shaped by past experiences. If "being noticed" has previously resulted in negative attention (for example abuse or bullying), you may currently be using body language that helps you remain invisible. If "being noticed" has previously resulted in positive attention (for example, through athletic performance or professional success), you may currently be using more assertive body language.

Women's Body Language

All too often, women adapt a passive body stance—that is to say, we use our posture, gestures, facial expression, and proximity in ways that communicate submission or fear. Know what you are saying with your body language.

For instance, women who are submissive tend to exhibit the following:

- Minimize their gate by walking one foot in front of the other, as though on a tightrope.
- Sit physically closed, with arms in, legs crossed, body hunched over.
- Employ the "head tilt" with mouth slightly open (a "Playboy pose").
- Gaze softly with big "Bambi" eyes, blinking frequently.
- Wear a soft smile.
- Laugh at comments that are not funny.[66]

I remember reading a book on photography published in the 1970s. The authors recommended that male subjects should look directly at the camera, but female subjects should have a softer glaze in their eyes and look at anything *except* the camera. Direct eye contact was considered aggressive and inappropriate for women. You can still find examples today where these principles are employed!

Whatever message you want to project, you're welcome to it, and I encourage you to do it consciously and with intention. Become aware of the signals you send. Play with them, and change them if needed.

Some of the more common physical "signals" that we send are listed below.

Body Language

	Assertive body language	**Passive body language**
Eye contact	Comfortable and direct	Not meeting the gaze
	Quick raising of the eyebrows upon greeting	Absent-minded gazing, infrequent blinking (zoned out)
		Staring
		Down and away or dropped glances
Mouth	Warm, smiling	Pursed, tightlipped, unsmiling
	Relaxed	Smiling at everything
	Uncovered (don't cover your mouth when you smile!)	Frequently swallowing
		Biting lips
Head	Head tilted while listening	Not fully facing, at an angle
	Nodding appropriately	Excessive nodding
	Chin up	Frozen, locked into position
		Chin into chest
Handshake	Firm grasp	Weak like a jellyfish
		None
Body	Open, inclusive gestures (palms showing)	Leaning away
	Fully facing others	Hunched shoulders
	Leaning forward Upright but relaxed posture	Too-stiff posture
	Feet firmly planted	Arms crossed or Legs crossed
	Sitting forward	Fidgeting
	Still and focused	

BEING INTENTIONALLY POSITIVE

Do you want to be happier?

If so, intentionally smile more often. Whether or not you feel like smiling doesn't matter! A smile will change your physiology and, in most cases, your overall mood. Try smiling when you're in a BAD mood and see what happens.

I remember an experience in a restaurant when I saw a fellow dining by himself, as happy as can be. The restaurant was crowded, and the tables were jammed together closely. This fellow was looking around, from right to left and everywhere in between, and whenever he caught someone's gaze, he would smile broadly and comment on how much he was enjoying his meal.

What do you think he attracted?

If you guessed smiles and warmth, you're absolutely right. As I sat at a table slightly off to his left, I could not help but to be drawn into his joy. I found myself smiling at him and at everyone he smiled at. I shared my compliments on the food and the restaurant with him. By projecting such fantastic warmth and happiness, he was spreading it around like crazy.

I don't know what his mood was prior to coming to the restaurant, but I would bet he was floating on a cloud of happiness when he left.

Think of how you react when someone's joy shines through above all else. Contagious, isn't it?

When you engage your smile more frequently, you will feel, reflect, and attract more happiness.

CALL TO ACTION

In keeping with the perpetual call to awareness, I want you to consider what confidence look like to you. What does a person who is confident physically project?

1. When you see someone who lacks confidence, how does she:

   a. Talk

   b. Walk

   c. Move her body

2. When you see someone who emanates confidence, how does she:

   a. Talk

   b. Walk

   c. Move her body

3. In order to emanate increased confidence (and grow it within yourself), how will you:

   a. Talk

   b. Walk

   c. Move her body

Chapter 10

REDEFINING FEAR AND FAILURE

The path to growth, confidence, and personal success can include many obstacles, and they may come from within you or from external circumstances.

Although usually the hardest to overcome, you will have more control over internal obstacles.

INTERNAL OBSTACLES

Doubt, fear, and self-deprecation—these are some of the more common sources of internal obstacles. What's most troubling is that we create them ourselves.

Children are typically naturally empowered and self-confident. They either *enjoy* what they are doing or they don't do it. Joyful, playful, and thoroughly loving life, they live completely in the moment. Children live in unspoiled wonder and amazement, are willing to explore everything, and have no fear of the unknown.

> *My life has been filled with terrible misfortunes—most of which never happened. Life does not consist mainly—or even largely—of facts and happenings. It consists mainly of the stormy thoughts that are forever blowing through one's head.*
> — Mark Twain

Toddlers are incredibly persistent. They keep trying to walk until they *can* walk. They have to fall again and again and again in the process, but they keep getting up and trying. (On the other hand, most adults are too afraid of failure and disappointment even to *try* something new, and if they "fail" at the first attempt, they never try again!)

Infants have only two inherent fears: a fear of falling and a fear of loud noises. All other *inauthentic* fears—failure, success, rejection, the unknown, judgment, inadequacy—are learned from our well-intentioned parents or from our environment.

What would happen in *your* life if you were to adopt a childlike belief in yourself? One without the obstacle of inauthentic fear?

EXTERNAL OBSTACLES

If your internal obstacles are those limiting beliefs (the doubts and fears and self-deprecation that come from within), your external obstacles are everything else. They range from extreme (the people who damage your self-esteem, the natural events like hurricanes, floods, and earthquakes that slam the brakes on progress) to mundane (a quarrel with a loved one, or a road closure).

The best way to overcome external obstacles is with clarity. Understand your vision. Know exactly what you're trying to do. Take the time to define your goals and the steps you intend to take to reach them.

Even with an exceptional plan, the reality is that things rarely go exactly as you expect. You'll have to stop and make changes at times, and that's okay. Be prepared for the unexpected; brainstorm ideas for handling problems if (or before) they arise.

Good planning and creativity will help you deal with external obstacles. Remember there are ALWAYS multiple ways to solve a problem.

FALSE EXPECTATIONS APPEARING REAL (FEAR)

What are your own "false expectations" that you have allowed to "appear as real"? For most of us, the top three fears are risk, rejection, and criticism. And also true for most of us is that the bulk of our fears are never actualized.

Winston Churchill once pointed out that "Ninety percent of what you worry about is unlikely to happen and of the remaining ten percent, ninety percent of those are likely but can usually be successfully navigated or averted." The bottom line is that only a small fragment of the fears we implant in ourselves are justified.

Can you think of a situation you were intensely worried about this time last year (or at your last job, or in your last relationship)? I suspect now you can barely remember the details. At a time when you experienced a justifiable fear that materialized, I'm willing to bet that you found your way through it.

There's a story that I often recall that helps me put my fears and intensely negative emotions aside. It's about building sandcastles.

In this story, there are a group of children building sandcastles on the beach. Each child is individually consumed in her or his own creation. Along comes wild and crazy Billy who takes it upon himself to smash down one of the finest and most elaborate of creations. The children collectively swarm Billy, knock him down and kick him till he is bruised all over and crying out from the pain. One participates because it was her sandcastle that was destroyed; the others kick in because theirs might have been next.

A few short hours later the day, as it always does, the trip to the beach comes to an end. The children have all gone home and are now focused on their evening mealtimes and nighttime rituals. The tide, as it does always and forever, comes in and washes away all remaining traces of the sandcastles.

What sandcastles are you currently fighting for?

PAIN/PLEASURE PURSUIT

Human beings are driven by two main motivators: to move away from pain and to move toward pleasure. Earlier in this book, you explored some of the negative stories that you held, or still hold, about yourself. Those are your pain motivators.

Sadly, many of us are motivated by pain. As noted earlier, 80% of our thoughts are negative, and as strange as it seems, we sometimes view intense pain as a durable existence.

Women in the abuse cycle are an obvious example of this. Domestic violence is an incredibly complex issue, as are the range of human emotions intertwined within it.

The following information comes from the National Coalition Against Domestic Violence.[66] It identifies the three main reasons why women stay in abusive relationships:

1. A lack of resources (she's a stay-at-home mom; she has no access to the joint bank account; she doesn't think she can get a job).

2. Sources that maintain a "better the devil you know than the devil you don't" attitude (especially those that emphasize "family" values).

3. Traditional thinking ("Single parenting is too hard; divorce is not an option; it's my fault").

Each of these belief systems creates self-imposed limitations and shapes the direction of her future.

> There came a time when the risk to remain tight in the bud was more painful than the risk it took to blossom.
> — Anais Nin

Pain motivators are not only in domestic violence situations. How many people do you know (perhaps yourself included?) who absolutely hate their jobs and are unwilling to leave them? They'll bitterly complain to their colleagues during their coffee breaks and begrudgingly do their work—or at least meet the absolute minimum requirements to keep from getting fired—but they won't consider quitting.

How many people do you know who absolutely hate the financial institutions with which they deal (or their accountant or hairdresser or whoever), but despite all their complaining, they will not move to another provider?

How many people do you know who continually say they need to get into better shape or lose weight yet they still maintain the same habits that brought them to their current state? How many smokers do you know who are aware of smoking's deadly risks?

When having to choose between the devil we know and the devil we don't, we tend to pick the devil we know—because we tend to believe there is a "devil" in taking risk. Perhaps our choice is really between the devil we know and the paradise we don't, or the devil we know and the success we don't. Our intense (and perhaps unjustifiable) fear of the unknown can keep us locked into the state of perpetual misery by holding close only what is familiar.

Pretty masochistic, wouldn't you say? In all too many cases, we never take the risk of change until the pain becomes overwhelming.

Many Large Group Awareness Training programs employ the intensification of personal pain, where intense (temporary) change is brought about in a relatively short period of time (a week or a weekend). Why? Because it works, at least temporarily. But that is akin to fad dieting as far as I am concerned. It's fast and furious, and you see results in the short term; but in the long term, you ultimately drift back to your previous habits.

Sure, sometimes it works. A man has a heart attack at 33 and changes his eating and exercise habits for life. But why wait for the extreme? Meaningful and lasting change comes from engaging change *before* the next trauma strikes. Plan it, state it, study it, envision it, build a team that will support you through it. Learn about entrepreneurship before you get fired. Discover your available resources and leave the relationship before the next near-death beating. The quick fix is a bandage, good for the short-term. Longevity comes from application through intent, not through trauma.

THE POWER OF FEAR

The first step in kick-starting initiative is to get inside your fear. According to Robert Gerzon, "[w]hen you boil down most of our fears and anxieties, what's left at the bottom is our fundamental dread about not having it our way. Every worry, every anxiety is a variation of this basic concern....As soon as we want things to be a certain way, we become anxious that they might not turn out that way."[68]

I attended a four-day personal development seminar attended by about 800 others (yep, my own experience with Large Group Awareness Training, or LGAT). At the beginning of the course, we gave the (group) vow to participate at 110% (impossible, but it makes the point; we were to commit fully). At the end of the fourth day, we did an exercise where we confronted fear.

First came the build-up. The training volunteers all entered the room in ceremonial garb, and each was holding an armful of real archery arrows, wooden dowels with rounded metal tips. They stood at the various exit doors all dressed in warrior costume, looking rather ominous. They were also equipped with latex gloves and protective eye-glasses.

Then came the disclaimer. Papers were distributed. Each participant was to sign a disclaimer stating that the training organization was not to be held responsible for any damages that might ensue in the following exercise.

Next came the instructions. We were to self-select ourselves into groups of eight or ten people. Each person would be given an arrow. After you briefly recalled your biggest fear, you were to write the name of that fear on the wooden part of the arrow.

We all had to put on the protective eye gear and the latex gloves. Blood had been shed in past events, we were told. Our apprehensions grew.

One person, typically one who had previously taken this course (there were a few repeat attendees), or the physically strongest in the group would be assigned as the group leader. That leader was to hold the end of the arrow flush against the palm of his hand. The other person, the participant, was to place the metal tip against the soft part of her throat (right in the dip of the collar bone).

Then, properly attired and surrounded by the group, the participant would remove her hands from the arrow. It was held up now only by the pressure from two human entities. Then, she was to take a deep breath, name her fear, and then step forward, into the arrow. The step had to be big and determined. Or else….

The objective, as they demonstrated to us from the stage, was to break the arrow.

The exercise began.

All around me was evidence, visual, concrete evidence of arrows snapping. No one was getting hurt. Even so, when my turn came, I was terrified to step into that arrow. What if mine didn't break? Just because multitudes of arrows were snapping all around me gave no guarantee that mine was indeed breakable. What if mine were the anomaly? What if I actually pierced my throat? What if I injured myself? Or worse?

My anxieties heightened, in spite of the obvious lack of fatalities (never mind injuries) around me.

When the exercise was over, I felt a sense of euphoria. I didn't die. I didn't even get a scratch. But I was incredibly impressed by the power my negative thoughts had held over me. Even with ample evidence that something inconceivable could be achieved, I doubted my ability to "pull it off." Were I given an opportunity to excuse myself from the exercise, I would have done so. But I was honor-bound by a four-day old commitment, and besides, the volunteers were all posted at the door.

And that is how fear works. We indulge ourselves with the thoughts of the most extreme negative possibility, and then we take those thoughts and (falsely) interpret them as our new reality.

Again, the beginning point of conquering fear is awareness. Become aware of the specific fear. Be aware of the thoughts that create the fear. Become aware of the excuses you engage in to avoid confronting them.

Fortunately, you are not the first person who has ever danced with her fears. You are not the first person ever to have stepped out of your comfort zone. That's where you mentors come in, and your network. They are the people who will support you, who will let you know that they too had fears and doubts, and that they too overcame them.

THE TOP FEAR: FAILURE

Getting over fears and navigating the abyss is many times easier said than done!

Now that you have identified your talents and the areas where you do—and will continue to—excel, we need to look at our own definitions of success and failure.

Fear of failure is often rephrased as "the fear of success," and truly they are the same thing. To achieve success, you must be able to fail repeatedly.

Winston Churchill said it best: "Success is going from failure to failure without loss of enthusiasm."

Here's a classic example.

A man worked as a chef at a restaurant. It was a busy restaurant that seated 142 people and served mostly travelers. Then the state built an interstate highway, which diverted traffic away from the restaurant, and the career of this once-popular chef was abruptly ended.

Instead of laying down his frying pan and giving up, this gentleman conceived a plan. He had a recipe for the most outstanding and flavorful deep-fried chicken. If he could sell his recipe for a portion of the proceeds of each sale, his retirement would be secured.

The gentleman, then sixty-five and with no savings and no retirement funds, hopped into his car and approached a multitude of restaurants with his idea. He used all of the $105 from his first Social Security check to fund his visits to potential franchisees.

The first restaurant turned him down. And another and another and another. Until over a thousand turned him down. Yet, he doggedly persisted.

For about a year, this man lived out of his car, driving from restaurant to restaurant, and pitching the same proposal to yet another prospect. Here was a man, incredibly committed to his idea. Failure was not an option, and he had the wisdom not to turn rejection into failure.

Take a note of that statement: Rejection is not the same as failure.

A rejection represents only someone's opinion. It does NOT represent a universal truth. Failure, true failure (not the kind you continually encounter enroute to success), is when you STOP. Everything else, as long as you're in motion, is part of the process of success in the making. This gentleman did not stop. He persisted through countless rejections.

Eventually somebody bought the idea.

> *Failure is impossible.*
> — Susan B. Anthony

Harland David Sanders, better known as Colonel Sanders, did manage to retire, thanks to the incredible success of Kentucky Fried Chicken. In 1964, he sold the business for $2 million dollars, and he continued to earn money by selling his image as the spokesperson for decades to follow.

Another tale of not giving up is the story of Florence Foster Jenkins, born in 1868. Her lifelong dream was to be a singer. Florence would not allow anything to get in the way of her dream.

Her wealthy father refused to pay for music lessons, so she eloped with a doctor and moved to Philadelphia. When her father died in 1909, she inherited his fortune.

This money allowed her musical career to skyrocket, and she would continue as an opera singer for thirty-two years. At the age of seventy-six, she gave her final performance at Carnegie Hall, the ultimate aspiration of many singers. She died a month after her last performance.

Here's the kicker: Florence Foster Jenkins was a bad, a *very* bad, singer.[69]

Don't confuse persistence with being able to achieve the impossible. Persistence enabled Jenkins to become renowned for her singing, even though a career as a *great* singer would be impossible.

When you know *what* you can achieve and what you can change, you can set out to make something happen.

REWRITING YOUR FEARS

Here is a simple and incredibly effective way to re-cast your fears into a more manageable, more realistic light.

First, think of one of your standard fears, one that prevents you from moving forward with a particular project or a dream.

Describe your fear in a simple sentence. This will be your Basic Fear Statement. Simply write something like: "I am afraid of _____." For example, you might write, "I am afraid of speaking in public," or "I am afraid of looking stupid in front of my peers/superiors."

You will notice how this sentence presents your fear as a sort of insurmountable entity.

Next, you're going to recast your Basic Fear Statement from an "I'm afraid of" statement to an "I want to" statement. Use this formula:

I WANT to	
	[state the same fear you outlined in your Basic Fear Statement]
and am concerned that	
	[these will list your true underlying fears and concerns]

When you list your underlying fears and concerns, be sure they reflect how your fear impacts you.

In this particular example, "fear of speaking in public," the writer might be concerned that other people will not listen, will not be interested, or will walk out of the room. Since she can't control other people, her NEW FEAR STATEMENT should be about her. If she's concerned that other people won't listen, are not interested, and will walk out on her presentation, the true underlying fears are about her performance: that she will run out of things to say, that she will appear stupid, etc.

Thus, her revised fear statement may look like this:

I WANT to	Speak in public
	[state the same fear you outlined in your Basic Fear Statement]
	I will run out of things to say
	I will stutter
and am concerned that	I will sound stupid
	[these will list your true underlying fears and concerns]

With this NEW FEAR STATEMENT, notice that what seemed like an insurmountable entity can be modified. Each of the underlying concerns can be addressed and resolved!

- If you fear stuttering, practice in front of a small audience, join Toastmasters, or sign up for other training.

- If you fear running out of things to say, be sure you have a well-prepared presentation.

- If you fear sounding stupid and uninteresting, be sure you know what you are talking about and that you are passionate about it.

Another way to reduce the magnitude of your fears is to simplify each fear. We can sometimes be consumed by the seeming largeness of our fears. For example, you dread speaking in public and you are assigned a presentation for next Monday. You (obviously) don't have the luxury of time to hone your skills through Toastmasters; you feeling a bit stressed out. Strike that. You are incredibly anxious and being hit by a bus would suit you just fine right now.

But before you step out in front of that bus, how about considering simplifying your fear? In a Senior's outreach manual by Tom Koziol (an unlikely place, I'll admit, but what a great find!), he talks about the importance of keeping things simple.

I'll paraphrase what he says, but essentially, his seven-step approach is this:

1. The situation exists. You have been assigned the presentation.

2. Accept it.

3. Determine what is NOT in your control, determine its importance, and then delegate or delete it. The time, perhaps, or the place. Are you preparing the speech yourself? Is somebody else? Who's doing the research?

4. Determine what is within your control and break down the things into small sizable chunks.

5. Start working on the small sizable chunks. Gather the facts to be presented. Outline the speech. Draft it. Practice it. Rewrite it. Present it to a colleague. Your job is only to focus on the task at hand.

6. Understand that you have ultimate mastery over the situation.

7. Know that you will succeed if you eliminate the complicated and keep it simple.[70]

Steps 1 and 2 are absolutely critical. As I continually say to my daughter (and as she also echoes back to me), "It is what it is." What you can alter is your response. Knowing what you can and can't change is key. Then, in setting out what you can change, it begins by taking little steps. As the sign outside a local gym says, "To finish first, you must first finish." A speech begins with an idea (or an assignment). A university degree begins with an application, and then a course. A business venture begins with an idea and then a plan. Think big, and then take little steps.

CHOOSING BETWEEN SUCCESS AND FAILURE

According to Princeton University's WordNet, success is defined as an "event that accomplishes its intended purpose."[71] Its opposite is failure. Failure is defined as an "act or instance of failing or proving unsuccessful."[72] Its opposite is success.

The metaphor we use when in a new project or undertaking often goes something like this:

1. You are standing at a crossroads.

2. You need to make a decision: should you turn right or left?

3. One road leads to Success; the other leads to Failure.

4. You venture down the road on your right.

5. You hit a roadblock, fall down, and land on your butt.

6. You get up again and decide that you have clearly picked the wrong road.

7. You go back to the original intersection.

8. If you're persistent, you start down the other road.

9. You hit a roadblock and again metaphorically fall down.

10. You decide that you have picked the wrong road.

11. You give up and go back down the road you came from because at least the universe was friendlier to you back there.

Any dominating idea, plan or purpose, held in the (conscious) mind through repetition of thought, and emotionalized with a burning desire for its realization, will be taken over by the subconscious mind and acted upon immediately by any natural and logical means available (to bring it to pass).
— Napoleon Hill

Now, what if you were to tweak the definitions of success and failure? Instead of offsetting them as polar opposites, what if you viewed them as collaborative terms. On your way from here to your dreams, you will encounter many failures, but each "failure" is a milestone to your inevitable success. As long as you are moving, you will be successful.

Interestingly, it is the accumulation of many failures that begets success. While you cannot guarantee that your destination will be exactly as you originally envisioned it, you *will* arrive at a destination. Ask anyone who has built a business. She had a vision in mind. She had clarity and a strong inclination to move in a particular direction, and she was continually surprised by what the final destination looked like.

To know what success means for *you*, it's critical that you understand and come to terms with the fact that failure is absolutely and necessarily what happens on the way to success.

Here is what some other great historic figures have said about success and failure:

- "Flaming enthusiasm, backed by horse sense and persistence, is the quality that most frequently makes for success." Dale Carnegie

- "I don't measure a man's success by how high he climbs but how high he bounces when he hits bottom." General George S. Patton

- "The person who gets the farthest is generally the one who is willing to do and dare. The sure-thing boat never gets far from shore." Dale Carnegie

- "To follow without halt, one aim; there is the secret of success. And success? What is it? I do not find it in the applause of the theater; it lies rather in the satisfaction of accomplishment." Anna Pavlova

> *TJust don't give up trying to do what you really want to do. Where there is love and inspiration, I don't think you can go wrong.*
> — **Ella Fitzgerald**

- "Many of life's failures are people who did not realize how close they were to success when they gave up." Thomas Edison

- "Success is never final. Failure is never fatal. Courage is what counts." Sir Winston Churchill

Think of how many people try business entrepreneurship and how few succeed at it. Those who "fail" do so, not because they "fell down," but because they stopped taking risks.

"True failure" (that is to say, the absence of success) only happens if you stop.

As long as you are **moving** with your dream in mind, you are **succeeding**.

CALL TO ACTION

Find and record your five favorite quotes about success, ones that inspire you to keep your eye on your goal and allow you to overcome any obstacle. Post them all over your house, carry copies with you in your wallet, and most importantly, LOOK AT THEM EVERYDAY.

Chapter 11

BECOMING UNSTOPPABLE

As you step out of your comfort zone and change who you are or how you do things, it is common to encounter resistance, which often comes in the form of discouragement, nay-saying, and doubting.

In the face of negativity, your job is to put it into proper context. People who love you may try to discourage you for one of two reasons (or possibly both):

1. They want to protect you from future harm.

2. They love you for who you are today, and they fear that you will leave them behind.

Even though it can be easy to say, "They are trying to hold me back," think about personal accountability. The only person responsible for your progress (or lack of) is you.

Take their opposition for what it is: a caring concern. Thank them, and keep on going! If you are now part of a mastermind group, it is the group's job to keep you focused on the positive, to support you through the doubts and fears you will battle from within and without.

Many people think that pursuing a dream is risky, but it is more risky to live your life—the one life you have been blessed with—according to the desires of well-meaning friends and family or concerned bosses.

In our hearts, we usually know why we have failed at something. All too often, we don't like to admit that truth to others, let alone ourselves. That's when we get buried in blaming and complaining.

The best advice I ever received was, "Live your life as though this were the *second* time, and now you have the opportunity to fix what was broken the first time around."

THE RIVER'S SOURCE AND DESTINATION

The metaphor I wish to draw upon here is that of a river. One thing that you might notice about any river is that it does not run in a straight line.

Very few things, in fact, run in a straight line. Switchback roads, for example, follow a winding path up and down the mountain's side. Much to the motorcyclist's delight, roads twist and turn. Rivers twist, turn, and meander.

Curves, as any woman will tell you, are natural.

Imagine you are on a drive across the mountains, and you've been on the road since early morning. At midday, you pull over for lunch.

There, just off to the left, is a bank that leads down to a gently flowing river.

You park the car and hike down to the magical spot. Now, standing at

the river's edge, you see some fish swimming in the waters, pushing playfully against the gentle current that pulls them downstream. A few water bugs skirt the water's surface, seemingly oblivious to the water's gentle pull.

You smell the slight pungency of the moist earth, the moss and forest. You put your hands in the fresh clean water, and you feel the current brush past. You hear the gentle

> *I finally figured out the only reason to be alive is to enjoy it.*
> — Rita Mae Brown

murmur of the water rumbling over and around the rocks and branches that lie gracefully in the path of travel.

And you can just about taste your picnic lunch.

STOP! Did you notice that this river is not flowing in a straight line! Something must be wrong with it!

Surely, if it were to follow our logical strategic project planning models, this river would have to be considered a failure, right?

1. First, you have where you are.

2. Then, you map your final destination (goal).

3. Then you figure out the five-year plan, the annual plan, the quarterly plan, the monthly strategies, the weekly play AND the daily schedule.

4. Then you determine milestones (the straight-line points between source and destination).

5. Then you begin, and measure yourself against this straight line.

6. Oh, and lest I forget, when you meander away from the line you either have to quit the project or shelve the strategic plan.

7. In fact right now, at the location you picked, the river's edge measures FURTHER away from the mouth or destination (429 miles) than the source ever did (356 miles).

Based on the "old" model of thinking, this river embankment would be considered a failure:

- It's further from the mouth than the source.
- It's not traveling in a straight line.
- It's way (and I mean waaaaay) off course.

Yet, that would be silly, wouldn't it? Why? Because the river is where it is for a very good reason, isn't it? The average person may not know what it is (although a geographer might), and it doesn't really matter. After all, here you are on this perfectly sunny day, by the river's edge, with your mouth-watering lunch.

The thought of stating a river is in the wrong place, as I have just described, is unlikely even to cross your mind. Rivers, trees, boulders, oceans, glaciers—all these natural events and bodies exist when and where it is most natural. Yet, we often berate ourselves for not being at the right place at the right time, not sticking to a plan, not staying on schedule. If we are not dead on track, we tell ourselves that we have failed miserably. We give up because "clearly it wasn't meant to be."

The river analogy is a great teacher. I use it with my students because it echoes a fundamental truth that we all inherently know, and yet, we consistently neglect to apply it to our own lives.

The lessons we learn standing at a river's edge are simple yet profound:

- You are never in the wrong place.
- There is always some value to where you are today.
- Going with the flow and working with what is will help you arrive at your destination sooner.
- You are neither good nor bad; you just are.

As long as you keep moving, you will arrive at your destination. Just as a river is unstoppable, so are you.

The New Goal-Setting Strategy

I'd like to toss the old model of goal setting out the window. Oh, sure, it has a place when you are trying to herd a flock of sheep from the pasture to the barn. But I suspect you are not a sheep, and your destination is bigger than the barn.

One of my many mentors, Bill Bartmann, gives a presentation on alternative goal setting that I find revolutionary. I will paraphrase here for you.

1. Before you even begin any mission for which you are going to put yourself on the line, make sure it is your goal. When goals are externally motivated (your mother tells you to clean your room), you are actually less likely to achieve it. When you are internally motivated (you clean your room because a friend is coming over and you want to impress her), success is probable.

   As a motorcycle instructor, the gauge I used to determine the most likely outcome for a student was to ask *for whom* they were learning to ride. One of my students suffered from a lack of confidence, which crippled her performance tremendously. She was literally shaking in the second exercise of the course, where she merely had to push the bike. At the end of the day, I asked her about her motivation. She was taking the course because it was her *husband's* goal to put her on her own bike. In fact, he wanted this so much for her that he had "kindly" bought her a Harley of her own. You can imagine the pressure this woman carried with her! When she realized that riding a motorcycle was not *her* goal or aspiration, she happily dropped out of the course.

   If you work toward a certain goal because your parents want you to, or your spouse wants you to achieve it, you will probably never achieve it. If you do, it will not bring you happiness.

In setting your goal, be sure that it engages your talent(s) and your passion, and make sure that the final result is measured *only* in your terms.

2. Don't call it a goal. Call it a promise.

We are subconsciously programmed to achieve a goal about 30% of the time. That means it is a whopping 70% of the time that we don't actually achieve the desired outcome! Think of how many New Year's resolutions you have managed to keep.

On the other hand, we're about 97% likely to keep our promises, according to Bartmann (who quotes a Harvard Medical School study). The message is clear. Don't set goals. Make (and keep) promises to yourself!

3. Clearly identify your promise.

The clearer you are on what your desired outcome will look, feel, sound, taste, and smell like, the more likely you are to achieve it.

- Use the tools (resources) around you.
- Tap into the power of collaboration. People who support you, who have complementary skill sets and additional contacts, are all around you. Ask for their guidance; they may be delighted to help you out. The more people (and other resources) with which you can collaborate, the more successfully you can keep moving toward your dream.
- Create a Promise Plan.

Your Promise Plan has six components:

Promises are the uniquely human way of ordering the future, making it predictable and reliable to the extent that this is humanly possible.
— Hannah Arendt

What: Be specific. Remember Napoleon Hill?

What are you promising to achieve? The clearer you are, the more likely it is to happen. Your "what" could be "to become a restaurateur" or it could be "to have a floating sushi restaurant that is also a registered bed and breakfast, in the harbor of my ocean-side villa."

By outlining and visualizing very specific directives, you are more likely to achieve the goal.

When: When will you complete your promise? What's your timeline?

It's one thing to say, "I will have my book written in two years"; it's quite another to say, "I will write three pages everyday for three months, report in weekly to my writers' group, and in exactly two years from today, I will have written, published, and marketed a book on women who drive race cars." Again, the emphasis is on clarity and specificity.

Where: Where do you see yourself once you have completed your promise?

What will life look like when you achieve your promise? Will you be doing speaking engagements? Online seminars? Will you be crafting your own seaside menu? Will you have a world class chef? What's the weather like? Wherever you are, what are you wearing? What are you doing? What kind of food and beverages are you drinking? How many hours per day and how many days per year are you working? The more you engage your senses in this part, the more anchored your promise will be in your psyche, and the more likely you are to achieve your dreams.

Why: Why are you doing this? Are you making this promise for yourself, or for somebody else?

Be clear on why you are making your promise. The more fully the "Why" resonates with your inner values, the more likely you are to achieve your promise.

Who: Who do you want on your team?

Who is with you? Who is against you? How can you leverage both groups to propel you forward?

How: How will you plan the next sixty-seven feet?

If the What and Why answers are clear, the "how" will come. Don't worry too much about the details, but DO focus on "the next sixty-seven feet." (Why sixty-seven? That's how far a car's low beams shine at night.) This is the metaphorical distance you can anticipate, move forward on, and react to.

4. Write it down.

Copy it many times (it's best to do so by hand so you *become* it), and post it all over your house. Put it in your wallet, your coat pockets, over the bathroom mirror and on the fridge. Go nuts! You cannot over-remind yourself.

5. Review the Promise Plan regularly.

Review your promise plan twice a day, for at least twenty minutes each time.

Tell yourself that ***you will succeed***. The movie, *What the Bleep Do We Know!?* makes the point that 95% of our thoughts are repeated, automatic thoughts. For a thought about your success to become automatic, you need to tell yourself again and again and again that you will succeed.

6. Tell others about your promise.

Anthony Robbins calls this "gathering leverage against your old habits and new ways." The more people you tell about your personal promise, the more bound you are to keeping it.

Envision the results.

Envisioning something ties into clarity. See yourself there, hear it, smell it, be it! Your brain cannot tell the difference between an intensely vivid emotional thought and what actually is. Once your brain believes it, the rest of you WILL follow.

7. Start. Act on the next sixty-seven feet.

You need to see with complete clarity your final outcome as well as the next sixty-seven feet. Without moving those next sixty-seven feet, you will never get anywhere. Take the first step. Start now.

Lastly, aim high. Shoot for the stars. You can shoot for the stars and land on the moon, or you can shoot for the streetlight and land at the end of your driveway.

YOUR PROMISE PLAN

Here is a sample Promise Plan as discussed in the previous section. Additional worksheets are included for your convenience in Appendix B.

Margaret's Promise Plan	
What	Write a book on how to grow peonies in your pesticide-free Zone 8 garden
	Eighty-five-page how-to guide
	Include regional waterfall graphs and organic gardening information
	Will generate an income of $15,000 per year, marketed both in hard copy and electronically
When	Book launch through Firefly Books Dec. 31, 2013 and online through Amazon
	Financial objective achieved Dec. 31, 2014
Where	On tour in the summer 2014
	At garden centers
	On vacation with the proceeds
	As the online expert

Why	Avid peony planter; have been teaching my friend my tips and tricks for three years. Can augment my retirement income. Can contribute to the beautification of my neighborhood AND earn money while doing it.
Who	My heroes: Martha, Jess, Amand, Singe, Nicole. Villains: Jared
How	Take chapter outline and create subheadings Read Peonies by Pamela McGeorge. Continue to research competitors and brainstorm my edge.

THE NATURAL PLANNING PROCESS

It's easy to be daunted by the words "strategic planning," but you needn't be. When I worked for larger corporations, I facilitated strategic planning sessions. They provided a great reason to get together with various departments and strategize about the future direction of the organization. We would produce reams of pages with valuable content: vision statements (the grand *raison d'être*), mission statements, goals, objectives, and milestones.

Invariably, the "bottom-line result was that the elaborate strategic plan would be filed in a big black binder and destined to gather dust for the next year or until the next strategic planning session.

Everyone knows how to plan the natural way. I was introduced to the following ideas about "natural planning" in David Allen's incredibly useful book, *Getting Things Done*.[73]

You go through a natural planning process with every "project"[74] you undertake. In this example, the "project" is going to a restaurant for dinner.

1. Define your purpose. (Notice how *everything* begins here?)

The first consideration is the reason for going out for dinner. It could be an anniversary, a birthday, or a retirement party. It may be as simple as the fact that you don't want to cook.

2. Envision the outcome. (Again, visualization continually asserts itself.)

Decide whether you're going to the local Mexican café or if you're ready for the five-star restaurant you've been dying to try for a few years. Whatever you choose, you will naturally see yourself eating there.

3. Brainstorm.

Come up with a list of people to invite and schedules to juggle. What night works best? This week or next? Do you need to find a babysitter?

4. Organize the results.

Decide responsibilities and what to delegate. Your spouse can find the babysitter and also has a connection with one of the restaurant owners. You have the contact list on your cell phone, so you should do the inviting.

Now transition from thinking and organizing to executing. Chunk it down. Define the steps and do them one at a time. Make the reservation, call the babysitter, arrange the transportation, arrive, and enjoy.

Before you know it, you are at the restaurant, eating dinner.

People can get overly fixated on the "How." With a natural planning process, you are not worried about potential roadblocks. The "why" is enough. You've made arrangements, you're committed, and whatever challenge springs up along the way, you know you can find an alternative.

THE HAT OVER THE WALL

I learned the "hat over the wall" technique at another personal development seminar offered by Brett Treadwell, founding member of Butterfly Global Inc. It goes something like this:

Imagine you have just bought the hat of your dreams and you paid $10,000 for this fabulous hat.

You are walking along a path, wearing this hat. You absolutely must reach your destination. Getting there is your life's purpose.

BAM! You run into a brick wall that extends as far as the eye can see. From where you stand, it looks like the Great Wall of China and is clearly impossible to scale.

What do you do next? You throw your $10,000 hat over the wall!

The lesson here is this:

1. You value your hat and are committed to your outcome.

2. You are committed to retrieving the hat no matter what.

3. It takes just one second to throw your hat over the wall.

What can you do in one second that will *commit* you to a future series of actions? What "hat" can you throw over the wall?

Anthony Robbins' Ultimate Success Formula includes these rules that I have adopted and live by:[75]

1. Have absolute clarity of your intended outcome. I can't stress this enough. Anyone who either studies Neurolinguistic

One of my students, Mary, wanted to write some online articles but had a hard time getting started. She decided to throw her "hat over the wall" by phoning one of her mentors, Veronika, whom she held in high esteem. Mary asked Veronika whether she would proofread a 350-word article on the following Wednesday. Veronika agreed. Though she had not yet conceived of or written the article, Mary was now committed to a series of actions.

Programming or has a vital aspiration can appreciate how critical it is to know what you want as your outcome.

Have you ever been at a job interview and been worried sick about how inadequate you were, how the employer wasn't likely to hire you, and how you really wanted the job? In 98% of these types of scenarios, you won't get the job.

Conversely, have you ever been at a job interview where you have been able to see yourself in that position, doing the job at that desk with the window seat, a photo of your family on the wall, your favorite tunes playing on your iPod, and smelling the fresh pot of coffee that just finished brewing?

To create the future you want, your vision of your desired outcome must be absolutely clear. Engage all your senses when you imagine it. What do you see? Smell? Taste? Hear? Feel?

2. Develop a hyper-keen sense of acuity.

    Develop and engage your sixth sense, your intuition, and learn to recognize when something moves you close to or further away from you goal.

    Don't worry about momentary obstacles. Remember, failure is defined only as a stepping-stone that moves you closer to success.

    Like a river, as long as you keep moving, you will never be at the "wrong" place. It will be just an AFGO (Another Frickin Growth Opportunity).

3. Be flexible.

    The popular writer and seminar leader Dr. Wayne Dyer often presents a set of common sense affirmations; one of them is to be open to everything and attached to nothing.[76]

This includes your attachment to the end result. Your Promise Plan needs to be reviewed daily (hence the postings throughout your house). See what still works and what doesn't, and modify your plan accordingly on a weekly basis.

In building the BNI business model, Misner developed a meeting structure that is proven to work. And, he says, a big part of the success of BNI is twofold: first is trusting what you know (accountability); second is trusting the knowledge and experience of others (collaboration). Misner is the first to say that the secret to success for running such a complex franchise (BNI) is that "you perform a balancing act between the stability of following a proven system and the importance of trying new ideas.... [T]he day you say, 'Look, this is the system, and you can't change a single thing under any circumstance'—that's the day you become number two."[77]

4. Take Action.

The mantra for real estate is "location, location, location." On the road to fulfilling your dreams, it's "action, action, action." Or in our case, initiate, initiate, initiate.

Chapter 12

PULLING IT ALL TOGETHER

YOUR FINAL CALL TO ACTION

The last word in the last chapter of this book will be yours, because as I've noted from the beginning, only you hold the key to your success. This book is intended to draw out the skills, knowledge, and resources that already exist within you. What you are going to do now is to write your epic saga.

Here are a few ground rules.

You are writing this saga for yourself—not for your mother's undying approval, not to win your partner's support, not to justify your existence to your colleagues. This one's for you. You are both the author and the central character, and as such, nothing is more important than you.

An epic story contains these eight characteristics:

1. Begin in the middle of your story. You have your past behind you and your future still to come.

2. Call upon a muse to inspire you. In ancient mythology, a muse was a female goddess or spirit that would inspire the creative process, and the author would be the spokesperson of her story. In modern terms, a muse is someone who inspires you and compels you

> *Our planet is filled with heroes, young and old, rich and poor, man, woman of different colors, shapes and sizes. We are one great tapestry. Each person has a hidden hero within, you just have to look inside you and search it in your heart, and be the hero to the next one in need. . . . [T]he hero in you is waiting to be unleashed. Serve, serve well, serve others above yourself and be happy to serve. As I always tell to my co-volunteers... you are the change that you dream as I am the change that I dream and collectively we are the change that this world needs to be.*
> — Filipino educator Efren Penaflorida in his acceptance speech for the CNN "2009 Hero of the Year" award

forward in your quest. Look over your list of mentors. Reconsider the people you most admire.

3. Main Character: Your main character is both yourself and an archetype, a generic version of a personality. She could be an Angel or a Warrior, a Detective or a Knight, a Trickster or a Professor.

4. The Plan: You have a statement of purpose. This is your cause, your *raison d'être*.

5. The Battle: You have opponents (people or groups who do not support your cause). These could be the naysayers in your life (who, as you remember, are acting from a place of caring but in a way that doesn't serve your growth). It could the failures you encounter en-route. Whatever or whoever your opponents are, you will encounter conflict. These will be your Dark Moments.

6. The Army: Your army is represented by the people in your network, your supporters, mentors, and guides. You are guided by a force greater than yourself. Consider your mastermind group here.

7. Your Self-Discovery: Your self-discovery usually occurs while you are outside of your comfort zone, while you are engaged in conflict and out of your element. It can also be referred to as an awakening. Here is where you finally see something that has been there all along.

8. Happily Ever After: You have a Triumphant Return.

Your saga is for exploration, not entertainment. Like all the exercises in this book, you are writing this piece only for yourself. This is yours to create. Take care and have fun.

> *Imagination is more important than knowledge.*
> — Albert Einstein

WRITING YOUR EPIC SAGA

Main Character's Name and Archetype:

Main Character's Purpose:

The Opponent(s):

The Plan:

The Battle:

The Army:

Self-Discovery:

Happily Ever After:

Epilogue

There's an ancient metaphoric monk's tale about accessing the divine. It goes something like this:

> You are walking through a forest when all of a sudden a tiger jumps out at you. You run as fast as you can, but the tiger gains ground quickly. You find yourself cornered at the edge of a cliff. The tiger has slowed to a menacing prowl, sensing that you are now an easy prey. You look over the edge. It's a drop of fifty feet. Your demise is inevitable. The tiger nears. Then you notice that halfway down the cliff there is a small outgrowth from a young tree, providing you with something to grab. A possible escape. The tiger is almost upon you now. You jump down and lunge for the young tree trunk. You grab it. Hanging there you contemplate the possibility of escape, it being now only half the remaining distance. You glance down. And to your incredible dismay, you see three other tigers down below, awaiting your inevitable descent.
>
> And then you notice it. There, just past where the tree has taken root in this small patch of earth is a strawberry. If you let go with one hand and reach as far as you possibly can, you might be able to get this one strawberry.

> *Character cannot be developed in ease and quiet. Only through experience of trial and suffering can the soul be strengthened, ambition inspired, and success achieved.*
> **— Helen Keller**

There, the story ends.

Some people will have you believe that you can have this most delectable, this most divinely tasting strawberry, without the risk, without the danger. But without this framework, the strawberry suddenly becomes just another strawberry. Nice, but not exceptional.

Other people will intentionally put you in front of the tigers and push you beyond your limits so you can taste the sweetness of the proverbial dangling carrot of hard cold cash. You are sure to see the tigers, but will the strawberry show up?

Neither of these will get you there.

Life is suffering. To quote the late poet, Gabrielle Bouliane, "You are going to die." You, me, and everyone we know.

Unstoppability cannot come from denying the existence of the tigers; nor can it come from intentionally stepping in front of the tigers. To deal with them, you need to see them coming. If your eyes are open and looking, the tigers are not difficult to spot. As long as you have the option, it is incumbent upon you to decide on a course of action. And sometimes, the only action that remains is to reach out for that strawberry.

Appendix A

FAMOUS FAILURES

I have included here a list of people and organizations that encountered abject failure and worked with limitations and challenges, yet they persevered and succeeded. They applied the principle of plowing through failures *in order to succeed.*

Louisa May Alcott was mostly home-schooled by her father. Poverty made it necessary that she work as a governess, teacher, seamstress, laundress, and live-in household servant.

Woody Allen was not a motivated student; he failed a film course at New York University and also failed English at N.Y.U. His now-famous screenplay *Annie Hall* was initially referred to as a "chaotic collection of bits and pieces that seemed to defy continuity."

Fred Astaire, according to Hollywood folklore, received the following judgment on a screen test report: "Can't sing. Can't act. Balding. Can dance a little."

Aunt Jemima went bankrupt.

Richard Bach took over ten years to write his 10,000-word story about a "soaring" seagull, *Jonathan Livingston Seagull.* Ready for the press, the manuscript was rejected by eighteen publishers before Macmillan finally published it in 1970. By 1975, it had sold more than 7 million copies in the United States alone.

Bachman-Turner Overdrive was rejected by twenty-four record companies.

The Beatles were rejected in 1962 by the Decca, Pey, Philips, Columbia, and HMV labels. Decca Records turned down a contract with the Beatles, saying, "Groups of guitars are on their way out."

Ludwig von Beethoven was deaf when he wrote some of his best music.

Alexander Graham Bell approached Western Union in 1876 and offered it exclusive rights to the telephone patent for $100,000. William Orton, Western Union's president, turned down the offer, posing one of the most shortsighted questions in business history: "What use could this company make of an electrical toy?"

Jack Benny was expelled from high school.

Leonard Bernstein was pressured by his father to give up his music and do something worthwhile, like help out in his family's beauty-supply business. Leonard Bernstein became a multi-Emmy-winning and Academy Award nominated American conductor, composer, author, music lecturer, and pianist.

Birds Eye Frozen Foods went bankrupt.

Robert Blake was once told that he could never learn to act.

Napoleon Bonaparte finished near the bottom of his class at military school, yet became one of the leading military men of all time.

Borden, the company famous for its dairy products, went bankrupt.

Andrew Carnegie only attended school for four years and started to work at two cents an hour.

Winston Churchill failed the sixth grade, and he had a stuttering problem as a child.

Christopher Columbus miscalculated the size of the globe and the width of the Atlantic Ocean and wound up discovering the island of San Salvador in the Bahamas (which he believed to be an island in the Indies), Cuba (which he thought to be a part of China), and the Dominican Republic (which he also mistook as part of the Far East).

Joan Collins, star of the long-running drama show "Dynasty," had a rather ironic initial assessment of her on-stage talents. It read: "Joan has a good personality and lots of stage presence. But she must try to improve her voice projection or she will wind up in films and TV, and that would be a pity."

Tim Conway's television series "Turn On" premiered on February 5, 1969, and was cancelled the same day.

Joan Crawford's starting salary was only twenty dollars a week when she worked as a dancer in a road show, which closed two weeks after it opened.

John Creasey, English Crime Novelist, published over 600 books (no one is sure exactly how many!) following 743 rejection slips. Since 1971, he has had worldwide sales of over 80 million copies in at least 5,000 different editions in twenty-eight different languages.

Glenn Cunningham suffered such severe burns when he was eight years old that the doctors told him he would never walk again and in fact recommended amputation. In high school, he was a champion athlete, and set a world high school record in the mile. He went on to become one of America's greatest runners, setting records and winning races with astonishing ease. In 1934, he set the World Record for the mile.

Daniel Defoe's book *Robinson Crusoe* was rejected by about twenty publishers before he finally got it printed.

Walt Disney started his own business from his home garage and his very first cartoon production went bankrupt. Walt Disney was fired by a newspaper editor who said, "he lacked imagination and had no good ideas."

Bob Dylan was booed off the stage at his high school talent show.

Clint Eastwood was once told by a Universal Pictures executive that his future wasn't very promising. The man said, "You have a chip on your tooth, your Adam's apple sticks out too far, and you talk too slow."

Thomas Edison was fired from his job working in a telegraph office after one of his experiments exploded.

Albert Einstein did poorly in elementary school, and he failed his first college entrance exam at Zurich Polytechnic. Aside from being only sixteen, two years below the usual age, the plain fact was he did not study for it. After graduating from the university, Albert Einstein had difficulty finding a post. He went through three jobs in a short time. His first job was as a temporary research assistant, the second as temporary replacement for a professor who had to serve a two-month term in the army. His third job as a teacher in a boarding school lasted for only a few months.

William Faulkner failed to graduate from high school because he didn't have enough credits. He later worked as a postmaster until he was fired for reading on the job. He tried writing and had five books finished by 1930 but failed to earn enough money to support a family.

Henry Ford's first two automobile companies (Detroit Automobile Company and Henry Ford Company, later renamed the Cadillac Automobile Company) failed.

Viktor E. Frankl was dismissed from the psychiatric society in Vienna, Austria, only to become a world respected, prominent psychiatrist.

Benjamin Franklin attended school for only two years.

Bill Gates was a Harvard University dropout.

Ruth Bader Ginsburg received no job offers when she graduated from law school. She now serves on the U.S. Supreme Court.

William Goldman was fired after writing his first screenplay. He is renowned in the industry as being the most intuitive screenwriter in the business, having written *Butch Cassidy and the Sundance Kid* and *The Princess Bride*, and the screenplay adaptation for *All the President's Men*.

Betty Grable was told by a ballet teacher to give up the idea of ever becoming a dancer.

John Grisham's first novel, *A Time To Kill*, was rejected by many publishers in 1987. He has since written over twenty other works of fiction and one non-fiction book, and has sold over 60 million copies of his books.

Frank Herbert's massive science-fiction tale *Dune* was rejected by thirteen publishers with comments like "too slow," "confusing and irritating," "too long," and "issues too clear-cut and old fashioned."

Bill Hewlett and **Dave Packard**'s (of Hewlett and Packard) early failed products included a lettuce-picking machine and an electric weight-loss machine.

Dustin Hoffman, while struggling to work as an actor in New York, worked as a janitor and an attendant in a mental ward.

Richard Hooker worked for seven years on his humorous war novel, *M*A*S*H*, only to have it rejected by twenty-one publishers before Morrow decided to publish it. It became a runaway bestseller, spawning a blockbuster movie and a highly successful television series.

Rock Hudson took thirty-eight takes to deliver one line of dialogue in his first movie, 1948's *Fighter Squadron*; he finally got it right, but only after the line was rewritten.

Joan of Arc was illiterate and a bit of a homebody.

Billy Joel, embarrassed by his first album, COLD SPRING HARBOR, spent six months playing bar piano in the lounge of the Executive Room in Los Angeles under the pseudonym Bill Martin.

Michael Jordan was cut from his high school basketball team when a sophomore.

Robert F. Kennedy flunked the first grade.

Gregor Johann Mendel (1822-1884) the Austrian botanist who discovered the basic laws of heredity, never was able to pass the examination to become a full-fledged teacher of science.

Laurence Olivier's first professional role was that of a policeman in a play called *The Ghost Train*. At his first entrance, the very first time he ever set foot on the professional stage—he tripped over the door-sill and fell headfirst into the floodlights.

Pepsi-Cola went bankrupt three times.

Elvis Presley tried to join his high school glee club but was turned down.

Quaker Oats went bankrupt three times.

Ronald Reagan was proposed for the lead role of the distinguished front-running presidential candidate. He was rejected because he lacked the "presidential look."

Carl Sandburg left school at age thirteen. He went back to school for only two weeks at West Point, and dropped out because he failed his math and grammar exams. He later entered Lombard College, but he left without a degree. In spite of his academic record, he did go on to win three Pulitzer Prizes, two for his poetry and one for his biography of Abraham Lincoln.

Colonel Sanders was rejected over a thousand times before someone would back his business. He started Kentucky Fried Chicken.

Charles Schulz was told by his high school's yearbook staff that his cartoons were not acceptable for the annual.

Sylvester Stallone was thrown out of fourteen schools in eleven years. His professors at the University of Miami discouraged him from a career in acting. His screenplay for *Rocky* was also rejected by all but one company, which insisted that if the company bought it, Stallone would not act in it.

James Thurber started writing sketches for the *New Yorker* in 1926, but the magazine kept turning him down (more than twenty times) before finally accepting a short piece on a man caught in a revolving door. Thurber never looked back. He published more than twenty books of collected prose and delightful pictures he drew himself.

Liv Ullman, two-time Academy Award nominee for Best Actress, failed an audition for the state theater school in Norway. The judges told her she had no talent.

Orville Wright was expelled from the sixth grade for mischievous behavior.

Wrigley's went bankrupt three times.

Appendix B

YOUR PROMISE PLAN

What	
When	
Where	

Why	
Who	
How	

Appendix C

RANDOM QUOTES FROM INSPIRATIONAL WOMEN

Great minds discuss ideas, average minds discuss events, small minds discuss people.
— **Eleanor Roosevelt**

I would venture to guess that Anon, who wrote so many poems without signing them, was often a woman.
— **Virginia Woolf**

Never interrupt someone doing what you said couldn't be done.
— **Amelia Earhart**

You take your life in your own hands, and what happens? A terrible thing: no one to blame. — *Erica Jong*

We cannot have a world where everyone is a victim. "I'm this way because my father made me this way. I'm this way because my husband made me this way." Yes, we are indeed formed by traumas that happen to us. But you must take charge, you must take over, you are responsible.
— **Camille Paglia**

Women must pay for everything.
They do get more glory than men for comparable feats.
But, they also get more notoriety when they crash.
— **Amelia Earhart**

The statistics on sanity are that one out of every four Americans is
suffering from some form of mental illness. Think of your three best
friends. If they're okay, then it's you.
— **Rita Mae Brown**

I have met brave women who are exploring the outer edge of human
possibility, with no history to guide them, and with a courage to
make themselves vulnerable that I find moving beyond words.
— **Gloria Steinem**

While they were saying among themselves it cannot be done,
it was done.
— **Helen Keller**

You gain strength, courage, and confidence by every experience in
which you really stop to look fear in the face. You must do the thing
which you think you cannot do.
— **Eleanor Roosevelt**

Many persons have a wrong idea of what constitutes true happiness.
It is not attained through self-gratification but through
fidelity to a worthy purpose.
— **Helen Keller**

Life is an opportunity, benefit from it.

Life is beauty, admire it.

Life is bliss, taste it.

Life is a dream, realize it.

Life is a challenge, meet it.

Life is a duty, complete it.

Life is a game, play it.

Life is a promise, fulfill it.

Life is sorrow, overcome it.

Life is a song, sing it.

Life is a struggle, accept it.

Life is a tragedy, confront it.

Life is an adventure, dare it.

Life is luck, make it.

Life is too precious, do not destroy it.

Life is life, fight for it.

—— **Mother Teresa**

Optimism is the faith that leads to achievement. Nothing can be done without hope or confidence.
—— **Helen Keller**

I finally figured out the only reason to be alive is to enjoy it.
—— **Rita Mae Brown**

The first problem for all of us, men and women, is not to learn, but to unlearn.
—— **Gloria Steinem**

There came a time when the risk to remain tight in the bud was more painful than the risk it took to blossom.
— **Anais Nin**

Failure is impossible.
— **Susan B. Anthony**

Promises are the uniquely human way of ordering the future, making it predictable and reliable to the extent that this is humanly possible.
— **Hannah Arendt**

Just don't give up trying to do what you really want to do. Where there is love and inspiration, I don't think you can go wrong.
— **Ella Fitzgerald**

Life is either a daring adventure or nothing at all. Security is mostly a superstition. It does not exist in nature.
— **Helen Keller**

Appendix D

ADDITIONAL ONLINE RESOURCES

Social Networking, Blogging Resources

For a comprehensive list of the hundreds of online networking sites, go to http://en.wikipedia.org/wiki/List_of_social_networking_websites; the list is both current and comprehensive.

Facebook: How-to-use-Facebook guide, Mahalo Web site
www.mahalo.com/how-to-use-facebook
Fifty ideas on how to use Twitter for business:
www.chrisbrogan.com/50-ideas-on-using-twitter-for-business
Twitter Glossary on the Twitter Fan Wiki:
http://twitter.pbworks.com/Twitter+Glossary
The Ten Rules of Twitter (and how the author Robert Scoble breaks every one of them): http://scobleizer.com/2007/09/23/the-10-rules-of-twitter-and-how-i-break-every-one
Twitter Style Guide as explained by Grammar Girl:
http://grammar.quickanddirtytips.com/twitter-style-guide.aspx
Automatic Updating sites (lets you update multiple social media sites with one entry): Ping.fm

The Top Blog Directory: Technorati.com

"Inhale the web" at addictomatic.com, where you can create a current custom page on any topic

Networking Resources for Women

Entrepreneur Journey Blog: www.entrepreneurs-journey.com

Femalepreneurs: www.femalepreneurs.com/blog

Mommy Millionaire: www.mommymillionaire.com

National Association of Women Business Owners:
www.nawbo.org

Startup Princess: http://startupprincess.com

Women Into the Network: www.networkingwomen.co.uk

Women's Funding Network: www.womensfundingnetwork.org

Women's Environmental Network: www.wen.org.uk

National Women's Health Network: www.nwhn.org

Women's Executive Network: www.wxnetwork.com

Other Resources

BNI: www.bni.com and www.bnipodcast.com

BNI podcasts, for free, at www.bnipodcast.com

A Complaint Free World (focused on promoting positive thinking).
www.complaintfreeworld.biz

I'm Allowed: www.imallowed.com

The Three Strategies of the Unstoppable Woman:
www.thethreestrategies.com

Think and Grow Rich, downloadable version is available at
www.namastecafe.com/download/ThinkAndGrowRich.pdf

Appendix E: Death Sentence

BY GABRIELLE BOULIANE

Some of you will know what I'm talking about here.

The ones of you quiet in the audience
who have had gun placed to their heads.

The one out of three women that have been raped.

People who have survived car crashes,
the victims of child abuse,
anyone anywhere who has had a death sentence imposed on them from
outside.

That moment where the world stops
and all the things you think are so important every day
fall away,
and it's all you can do to whisper a prayer
for your parents
your lover

your children.

You get this one moment to regret

all the things you'd said you do but never did

and then it's over.

You die or you live.

If you live, the look in your eyes is never the same.

And when the normal people around you complain

about how terrible some slight on their ego is,

All you can do is smile and even be thankful that there are people out there who don't know how precious life is

Not to be wasted on such bullshit.

Cancer is like that.

One minute, everything is normal.

You're worried about paying the bills,

what your boss said at work that day,

if you'll ever loose that weight

take that class

get that job

toy

dress

man

whatever

And the next thing you know some stranger in a lab coat is telling you your life expectancy is less than a year.

And nothing is the same

ever again.

You think you have problems, but things can always be worse.

I kept a photo of a woman being wrapped

after a radiation treament from breast cancer

over my desk for 10 years

To remind me when I got sad or upset that I didn't have any right to complain.

Until I joined this sister.

And while I may have both my breasts

and my hair (at least for now),

I think: I've had to give up my job my apartment my car.

  My parents take care of me.

  I'm on 16 kinds of pills.

  I have to inject myself twice daily with blood thinners

  to make sure no more clots might slip up to my brain.

  I can't worry anymore about imagined offenses someone might have made.

  I can't fuss about not being properly kissed for the last two-and-a-half years.

  I can't pretend I'll be the next Terintino or J.K. Rowling.

Most days, my job is breathing,

making sure I have enough calories.

I've gone from selling a TV show to having a bowel movement
be the biggest event of my day.

Morphine is just asperin to me,
and I could tell you the best way to the hospital cafeteria
from the infusion center
the pharmacy
or the lab.
And it might be true,
Maybe I won't live until next September.
And you know what makes you different from me?
One blood clot.
One defective gene.
Maybe that cigarette or the next beer you drink
your liver will finally give up on you as well.
We never know when it's going to come.

So I ask you tonight:

What are you waiting for?
Why are you not being everything you can be right now?
Why haven't you asked that crush you have out on a date,
or applied for your motorcycle licence
or told your family you're going back to school to become the one career
you've always wanted to become (Thelida)
Whether it's sensible or not?

I know,

You've heard it a thousand times:

You only get one life.

Let me rephrase if for you in a way that will make more sense:

You're gonna die.

Sometime.

Some how.

The only difference between me and you is that I may have an idea of when and how.

And I'm lucky, you know.

I get to tell my parents I love them every day.

I get to say goodbye to everyone.

I'm in hospice.

I'll never be in pain.

I'll just drift away like a feather in a dream some day.

While you're stuck in traffic,

going to a job you never liked,

cursing the people around you,

Dreaming your "If only's."

Please.

Take it from a girl who's already half angel:

  Do.

  Not.

  Wait.

If you don't start today,
  get the fuck up,
  walk out that door,
  and change your life to the best it can be
then when?

Are you hearing me?

Don't wait for that moment when you almost loose your life;
Don't you dare waste your fucking time.

I'll be watching
Whether from the front row or from somewhere a little higher.

I've got your wings.
I'm keeping them right here.
The only price is letting go of your irrational fears.
I got them right here.
Come.
Find them.

Gabrielle Bouliane, at the Austin Poetry Slam 12.05.09

Watch Gabrielle Bouliane at www.youtube.com/watch?v=gePQuE-7s8c

BIBLIOGRAPHY

SELECT BOOKS

Allen, David. *Getting Things Done: The Art of Stress-Free Productivity*. New York: Penguin Books, 2001.

Amen, Daniel G., M.D. *Change Your Brain, Change Your Life*. Random House: New York, 1998.

Canfield, Jack. *The Success Principles: How to Get From Where You Are to Where You Want to Be*. New York: Harper Collins, 2005.

Chesler, Phyllis. *Woman's Inhumanity to Woman*. New York: Thunder's Mouth Press/Nation Books, 2001.

Covey, Stephen S. *The Seven Habits of Highly Effective People*. New York: Simon and Schuster, 1989.

Einstein, Albert. *Autobiographical Notes* (Centennial ed.). Chicago: Open Court, 1979.

Frank, Stephanie. *The Accidental Millionaire*. Scottsdale, AZ: Greenlight Publishing, 2006.

Frankl, Viktor. *Man's Search for Meaning*. New York: Simon & Schuster/ Touchstone, 1984.

Gardner, Howard. *Frames of Mind: The Theory of Multiple Intelligences.* Tenth Anniversary edition. New York: Basic Books, 1983.

Gerzon, Robert. *Finding Serenity in the Age of Anxiety.* New York: Bantam Books, 1998.

Godin, Seth. *Tribes.* New York: Penguin, 2008.

Hafiz. *The Gift.* Trans. by Daniel Ladinsky. New York: Penguin Books, 1999.

Hill, Napoleon. *Think and Grow Rich.* 1937. New York: Fawcett Crest. Revised Ed. (Hardcover), 1960.

Misner, Ivan R. with Jeff Morris. *Givers Gain: The BNI Story.* Upland, CA: Paradigm Publishing, 2004

Paglia, Camille. *Sex, Art, and American culture: Essays.* New York: Vintage, 1992.

Pelzer, Dave. *A Child Called It.* Deerfield Beach, Florida: Health Communications, Incorporated, 1995.

Plato. *The Republic.* Online version available through the Gutenberg Project at http://www.gutenberg.org/etext/1497.

Robbins, Anthony. *Unlimited Power.* New York: Random House, 1986.

Schwartz, David J. *The Magic of Thinking BIG.* New York: Prentice-Hall, 1959. Reprinted 1977.

Tolle, Eckhart. *A New Earth: Awakening to Your Life's Purpose.* New York: Penguin, 2005.

Vanzant, Iyanla. *Don't Give It Away!* New York: Simon & Schuster, 1999.

Williams, Roy H. *Magical Worlds of the Wizard of Ads.* Marietta, GA: Bard Press, 2001.

ARTICLES AND ONLINE SOURCES

Beauchemin, Eric. "Sexual Violence: Weapons of War." Radio Netherland Wereldomroep. http://static.rnw.nl/migratie/www.radionetherlands.nl/specialseries/women-war/warcrime-rape-redirected 18 December 2007. Extracted on October 26, 2009.

Brogan, Chris. "Fifty ideas on how to use Twitter for business." http://www.chrisbrogan.com/50-ideas-on-using-twitter-for-business

Carey, Benedict. "Snake Phobias, Moodiness And a Battle in Psychiatry." Health section of the *New York Times*. June 14, 2005. Online version available at http://query.nytimes.com/gst/fullpage.html?res=940CE1D E1F38F937A25755C0A9639C8B63&sec=health&spon=&pagewant ed=1. Extracted January 20, 2010.

de Brouwer, Anne-Marie. *Supranational Criminal Prosecution of Sexual Violence*. Intersentia. (2005) p. 11. http://books.google.co.uk/books? id=JhY8ROsA39kC&dq=war+rape+in+ancient+times&source=gbs_ summary_s&cad=0. Extracted January 1, 2010

Kaziol, Tom. "Care, Giving and Receiving: Nurturing in the Age of Aging." A Publication of Senior Outreach Ministries ©2004. p. 24. At the time of writing, the Senior's Outreach Manual by Tom Kaziol was available at http://www.katrinadisability.info/PDFsK/care.pdf (November 13, 2009).

Logan, David. "On Tribal Leadership." http://www.ted.com/talks/david_logan_on_tribal_leadership.html; another excellent summary of Logan's view is offered on a blog called The Mouse Trap, at http://the-mouse-trap.com/2009/11/07/the-five-tribal-stages/

Management Consulting News, interview with Rosabeth Moss Kanter, "Meeting the MasterMinds: Rosabeth Moss Kanter on Confidence" (date unknown) www.managementconsultingnews.com/interviews/kanter_interview.php. Extracted January 4, 2010.

Martin, Daniel. "Why women find it harder working for a Queen Bee than a male boss." MailOnline. Last updated at 9:56 AM on 23rd September 2008. http://www.dailymail.co.uk/femail/article-1059997/Why-women-harder-working-Queen-Bee-male-boss.html. Extracted on January 11, 2010. Read more: http://www.dailymail.co.uk/femail/article-1059997/Why-women-harder-working-Queen-Bee-male-boss.html#ixzz0cNYcodHG

McVeigh, Tracy. "It's no joke. We laugh to impress our bosses." *The Observer.* http://www.guardian.co.uk/uk/2000/oct/08/tracymcveigh.theobserver October 8, 2000.

Moore, David W. "About Half of Americans Reading a Book," Gallup. June 3, 2005. http://www.gallup.com/poll/16582/about-half-americans-reading-book.aspx

Robinson, Sir Ken. "Schools Kill Creativity." http://www.ted.com/talks/ken_robinson_says_schools_kill_creativity.html

Sarler, Carol. "Beware the Queen Bee boss—she's hell to work for (and I should know, I was one!), says Carol Sarler." Mail Online. Last updated at 12:43am on 25th September 2008. http://www.dailymail.co.uk/femail/article-1061416/Beware-Queen-Bee-boss--shes-hell-work-I-know-I--says-Carol-Sarler.html. Extracted January 11, 2010. Read more: www.dailymail.co.uk/femail/article-1061416/Beware-Queen-Bee-boss--shes-hell-work-I-know-I--says-Carol-Sarler.html#ixzz0cNa2Q0GN

Stirland, Sarah Lai. "Propelled by Internet, Barack Obama Wins Presidency." *Wired.* November 4, 2008, from http://www.wired.com/threatlevel/2008/11/propelled-by-in/

Taylor, Jill Bolte. "A Stroke of Insight." www.ted.com/talks/jill_bolte_taylor_s_powerful_stroke_of_insight.html. Taylor has a book out under the same title, *A Stroke of Insight.*

Taylor, Shelley E., Laura Cousino Klein, Brian P. Lewis, Tara L. Gruenewald, Regan A. R. Gurung, and John A. Updegraff. "Biobehavioral

Responses to Stress in Females: Tend-and-Befriend, Not Fight-or-Flight." *Psychological Review.* Los Angeles: University of California, 2000. Vol. 107, No. 3, p. 411-429.

United Nations. "A Human Rights and Health Priority." United Nations Population Fund. http://www.unfpa.org/swp/2000/english/ch03.html. Retrieved August 15, 2007.

Venutolo, Anthony. "Henry Winkler tells kids how he copes with a learning disability: 'One...word...at...a...time'." Article posted April 06, 2009, 4:43pm. http://www.nj.com/parenting/ben_horowitz/index. ssf/2009/04/henry_winkler_tells_kids_how_h.html. Retrieved October 7, 2009.

Wikipedia. "Florence Foster Jenkins." *Wikipedia, The Free Encyclopedia.* 9 Nov 2009, 06:13 UTC. <http://en.wikipedia.org/w/index. php?title=Florence_Foster_Jenkins&oldid=324794652>. Retrieved 13 Nov 2009.

Winkler, Henry. CBC Interview on the radio show, "Q" October 7, 2009. http://podcast.cbc.ca/mp3/qpodcast_20091007_21265.mp3

Wiseman, Professor Richard (University of Hertfordshire), "The loser's guide to getting lucky." BBC News. Monday, December 22, 2003. http://news.bbc.co.uk/2/hi/3335275.stm

Women's Web. "Domestic Violence: Why do women stay? Why don't they leave?" http://www.womensweb.ca/violence/dv/leave.php. Extracted October 19, 2009.

Movies

The Secret. Dir. Drew Heriot. TS Production, 2006. With Rhonda Byrne.

What the Bleep Do We Know!?: Down the Rabbit Hole. Dir. Betsy Chassee et al. Twentieth Century Fox, 2006. With Marlee Matlin.

References

1. Hafiz. The Gift. "To Build a Swing." Translated by Daniel Ladinsky. New York: Penguin Books, 1999. p. 48. *All poems by Hafiz are reprinted with permission.*

2. David Logan on TED tv at http://www.ted.com/talks/david_logan_on_tribal_leadership.html; another excellent summary of Logan's views is offered on a blog called The Mouse Trap at http://the-mouse-trap.com/2009/11/07/the-five-tribal-stages/

3. David J. Schwartz, The Magic of Thinking BIG. New York: Prentice-Hall, 1959. Reprint 1977. p. 54.

4. Professor Richard Wiseman (University of Hertfordshire), "The losers guide to getting lucky." BBC News. Monday, December 22, 2003. http://news.bbc.co.uk/2/hi/3335275.stm

5. Paglia, Camille. Sex, Art, and American Culture: Essays. New York: Vintage, 1992. p. 63.

6. Paglia, Camille. Sex, Art, and American Culture: Essays. New York: Vintage, 1992. p. 64.

7. Iyanla Vanzant. Don't Give It Away! New York: Simon and Schuster, 1999. p. 38.

8. Daniel G. Amen, M.D. Change Your Brain, Change Your Life. New York: Random House, 1998. p. 154

9. Daniel G. Amen, M.D. Change Your Brain, Change Your Life. New York: Random House, 1998. p. 172-185

10. Anthony Robbins. Unlimited Power. New York: Random House, 1986. p. 58-61.

11. Jack Canfield. The Success Principles: How to Get From Where You Are to Where You Want to Be. New York: Harper Collins, 2005. p. 6.

12. Which is closely modeled after Anthony Robbins' model of Belief→Potential→Action→Result, in the book Unlimited Power p. 65.

13. Sam Harris. *The End of Faith.* New York: W.W. Norton & Company, 2004. p. 12.

14. Robert Gerzon. *Finding Serenity in the Age of Anxiety.* New York: Bantam Books, 1998. p. 116.

15. Viktor Frankl. *Man's Search for Meaning.* New York: Simon & Schuster/Touchstone, 1984. p. 147.

16. Robert Gerzon. *Finding Serenity in the Age of Anxiety.* New York: Bantam Books, 1998. p. 107.

17. Daniel G. Amen. *Change Your Brain Change Your Life.* New York: Random House, 1998. p. 64.

18. Eckharte Tolle. *A New Earth: Awakening to Your Life's Purpose.* New York: Penguin (Dutton), 2005. p. 63.

19. I'm guilty on both counts. While I *despised* the playground, I *loved* the actual classroom. I learned soon enough that I *hated* the working-for-minimum-wage world, and after three years of no raises, I scurried back to the classroom.

20. Shortly after writing this section, I had a dream that I went for a job interview. I got the job in my dream, but what clinched it for me was my stating, as a last ditch appeal to be considered, that I had completed my master's degree with an overall 80%+ average. And that got me the job! I woke up smiling at the ridiculousness of that scenario.

21. Some say the shelf-life of a degree ranges anywhere from about eighteen months to five years, depending on the degree and the institute where it was given. My degrees are incredibly obsolete by now, but my education continues.

22. Einstein, Albert . *Autobiographical Notes* (Centennial ed.). Chicago: Open Court, 1979. p. 48–51.

23. This information comes from listening to an interview with Henry Winkler on the CBC Radio show, "Q" October 7, 2009. If it's still available, you can download the podcast at http:// podcast.cbc.ca/mp3/qpodcast_20091007_21265.mp3

24. "Henry Winkler tells kids how he copes with a learn- ing disability: 'One...word...at...a...time'," Anthony Venutolo, Article posted April 06, 2009, 4:43pm. http://www.nj.com/parenting/ben_horowitz/index. ssf/2009/04/henry_winkler_tells_kids_how_h.html Article retrieved on October 7, 2009.

25. Napoleon Hill. *Think and Grow Rich.* New York: Fawcett Crest Press, 1963. p. 57.

26. On TED.com, Sir Ken Robinson makes a similar argument, stating that today's educational system seeks only to educate from the waist up, while it neglects a multitude of other legiti- mate areas of genius. His is a highly entertaining and profoundly moving presentation, available at http://www.ted.com/talks/ ken_robinson_says_schools_kill_creativity.html

27. She then has the reader create a statement around what each value means specifically for you. For example, being of service can mean many different things. Each value has a corresponding statement. If this exercise appeals to you, I highly recommend you pick up a copy of Stephanie Frank's book, *The Accidental Millionaire*.

28. Robert Gerzon. *Finding Serenity in the Age of Anxiety*. New York: Bantam Books, 1998. p. 220.

29. The Seven Habits, briefly, are thus:

- Be Proactive
- Begin with the End in Mind
- Put First Things First
- Think Win-Win
- Seek First to Understand, THEN to be Understood
- Synergize
- Sharpen the Saw

Stephen S. Covey. *The Seven Habits of Highly Effective People*. New York: Simon and Schuster, 1989.

30. Robert Gerzon. *Finding Serenity in the Age of Anxiety*. New York: Bantam Books, 1998. p. 202.

31. Seth Godin. *Tribes*. New York: Penguin, 2008. p. 108.

32. Napoleon Hill. *Think and Grow Rich*. New York: Fawcett Crest Press, 1963. p. 36. The Definite Major Purpose (p. 20) goes by many names in his book, including "Definite Purpose" (p. 21), Definiteness of Purpose (p. 38, 157), and Definite Chief Aim (p. 55). For the purpose of clarity in this book, I'll reference it only as the Definite Major Purpose.

33. Shelley E. Taylor, Laura Cousino Klein, Brian P. Lewis, Tara L. Gruenewald, Regan A. R. Gurung, and John A. Updegraff. "Biobehavioral Responses to Stress in Females: Tend-and-Befriend, Not Fight-or-Flight." *Psychological Review*. Los Angeles: University of California, 2000. Vol. 107, No. 3, p. 411-429.

34. Daniel Martin. "Why women find it harder working for a Queen Bee than a male boss." MailOnline. Last updated at 9:56 AM on 23rd September 2008. http://www.dailymail.co.uk/femail/article-1059997/Why-women-harder-working-Queen-Bee-male-boss.html. Extracted on January 11, 2010. Read more: http://www.dailymail.co.uk/femail/article-1059997/Why-women-harder-working-Queen-Bee-male-boss.html#ixzz0cNYcodHG

35. Carol Sarler. "Beware the Queen Bee boss—she's hell to work for (and I should know, I was one!), says Carol Sarler." Mail Online. Last updated at 12:43 AM on 25th September 2008. http://www.dailymail.co.uk/femail/article-1061416/Beware-Queen-Bee-boss--shes-hell-work-I-know-I--says-Carol-Sarler.html. Extracted January 11, 2010. Read more: http://www.dailymail.co.uk/femail/article-1061416/Beware-Queen-Bee-boss--shes-hell-work-I-know-I--says-Carol-Sarler.html#ixzz0cNa2Q0GN

36. "Reena Virk's short life and lonely death," *The Globe and Mail*, 27 November 1997. For a brief overview, see the Wikipedia article. "Murder of Reena Virk," (2010, January 3). In *Wikipedia, The Free Encyclopedia*. Retrieved 07:11, January 12, 2010, from http://en.wikipedia.org/w/index.php?title=Murder_of_Reena_Virk&oldid=335686386

37. Phyllis Chesler. *Woman's Inhumanity to Woman*. New York: Thunder's Mouth Press/Nation Books, 2001.

38. Parrott, W. G., & R. H. Smith. "Distinguishing the experiences of envy and jealousy." *Journal of Personality and Social Psychology*, (1993) 64, p. 906-920. Popular culture uses the word jealousy as a synonym for envy. Many dictionary definitions include a reference to envy or envious feelings. Although popular culture often uses jealousy and envy as synonyms, modern philosophers and psychologists have argued for conceptual distinctions between jealousy and envy. For example, philosopher John Rawls distinguishes between jealousy and envy on the ground that jealousy involves the wish to keep what one has, and envy the wish to get what one does not have.

39. Russell, Bertrand. *The Conquest of Happiness.* New York: H. Liverwright, 1930.

40. Benedict Carey, "Snake Phobias, Moodiness And a Battle in Psychiatry." Health section of the *New York Times.* June 14, 2005. Online version available at http://query.nytimes.com/gst/fullpage.html?res=940CE1DE1F38F937A25755C0A9639C8B63&sec=health&spon=&pagewanted=1 extracted January 20, 2010.

41. Napoleon Hill. *Think and Grow Rich.* New York: Fawcett Crest Press, 1963. p. 168-9.

42. W. David W. Moore. "About Half of Americans Reading a Book," Gallup. June 3, 2005. http://www.gallup.com/poll/16582/about-half-americans-reading-book.aspx

43. Jason Hanna. "Good, bad and ugly self-help: How can you tell?" CNN. December 7, 2009.

44. Napoleon Hill. Think and Grow Rich. New York: Fawcett Crest Press, 1963. p. 169.

45. A copy of this nineteen-page eBook can be found online at http://www.thethreestrategies.com

46. Roman (Greek-born) slave & Stoic philosopher (55 AD - 135 AD)

47. Roy H. Williams. *Magical Worlds of the Wizard of Ads*. Marietta, GA: Bard Press, 2001. p. 50.

48. From http://en.wikipedia.org/wiki/Six_degrees_of_separation in the section on Computer Networks.

49. Sarah Lai Stirland. "Propelled by Internet, Barack Obama Wins Presidency." *Wired*. November 4, 2008, from http://www.wired.com/threatlevel/2008/11/propelled-by-in/

50. "About Us." LinkedIn Website. http://press.linkedin.com/about extracted November 4, 2009.

51. This book is now in the public domain and can be accessed through Project Gutenberg at http://www.gutenberg.org/etext/4507

52. Robert Gerzon. *Finding Serenity in the Age of Anxiety*. New York: Bantam Books, 1998. p. 108.

53. Most commonly attributed to the theologian Reinhold Niebuhr.

54. The funniest claim I've heard was that defying the Law of Attraction would be like defying the law of gravity in that it would produce awful results. Of course, the law of gravity is immutable and as such *cannot* be defied. I cannot wake up one morning and before I roll out of bed decide that today's the day I will not "abide" by the law of gravity. If the Law of Attraction were indeed immutable, I would not have to pay a guru $5,000 per consultation in order to apply it successfully to my life. I haven't consulted anyone, yet I have still managed to master the law of gravity....Don't get me started!

55. PRWeb (September 21, 2006). "Self-Improvement Market in U.S. Worth $9.6 Billion." Press release. http://www.prwebdirect. com/releases/2006/9/prweb440011.php. Retrieved 2008-12-18. "Marketdata Enterprises, Inc., a leading independent market research publisher, has released a new 321-page market study entitled: The U.S. Market For Self-Improvement Products & Services."

56. The excerpt in this book is printed with permission from Lakhani. The full interview can be heard on Michael Lovitch's blog Exploring the Mind, at http://exploringthemind.com/ how-to-protect-yourself-from-coercive-groups-and-leaders/

57. The following comes from Wikipedia, and is a summary of many news articles that can be found online. "James Arthur Ray." *Wikipedia, The Free Encyclopedia.* 16 Nov 2009, 22:40 UTC. Extracted 21 Nov 2009 <http://en.wikipedia.org/w/index. php?title=James_Arthur_Ray&oldid=326239813>.

On October 8, 2009, at a New Age "Spiritual Warrior" retreat conceived and hosted by Ray at the Angel Valley Retreat Center in Yavapai County near Sedona, Arizona, two participants of a sweat lodge exercise; James Shore and Kirby Brown died. Eighteen others were hospitalized after suffering burns, dehydration, breathing problems, kidney failure or elevated body temperature. Liz Neuman, another attendee, died October 17 after being comatose for a week.

The attendees, who had paid up to $10,000 to participate in the retreat, had fasted for thirty-six hours during a vision quest exercise before the next day's sweat lodge. During this vision quest, participants were left alone in the Arizona desert with a sleeping bag, although Ray offered them Peruvian ponchos for an additional $250. After this experience, participants ate a large buffet breakfast before entering the sweat lodge. A site owner reported she learned after the event that participants went two days without water before entering the lodge.

58. If you are interested in hearing the story of the survivor of an intense stroke, I urge you to listen to Jill Bolte Taylor's presentation on TED tv at http://www.ted.com/talks/jill_bolte_taylor_s_powerful_stroke_of_insight.html; she has a book out under the same title, *A Stroke of Insight*.

59. This story is not an original, and there are many iterations of it online.

60. Fast-ball pitches can travel anywhere from 88–97 miles per hour after all; curve balls are a bit slower in the 74–88 mph range; sliders can run anywhere from 84–91 mph, and the slowest is the knuckle ball, thrown at about 55–75 mph. You'd have to be fearless to stand in front of that! Stats extracted from http://wiki.answers.com/Q/What_is_the_average_pitching_speed_in_MLB on November 24, 2009.

61. Robert Gerzon. *Finding Serenity in the Age of Anxiety*. New York: Bantam Books, 1998. p. 132-3

62. Gerzon prefers the term "anxiety" to "fear." All fears begin as anxieties (*Finding Serenity in the Age of Anxiety* p. 14), and it's how you respond to that fear that determines the classification of anxiety. A "real" fear, such as a mugger attacking you on the street, is referred to as a Natural Anxiety (this is the kind of fear that Gavin de Becker writes about in his book, *The Gift of Fear*. It is an actionable fear with a course of action that produces results, whether positive or negative, in the moment. A fear that results in destructive anticipatory thoughts of "anxiety, agitation, apprehension, worry, nervousness, depression, grief, dread, terror and panic" (p. 14) is referred to as Toxic Anxiety. A fear that results in personal development, growth, and fulfillment is referred to as Divine Anxiety.

63. Robert Gerzon. *Finding Serenity in the Age of Anxiety*. New York: Bantam Books, 1998. p. 135

64. Plato. *The Republic*. Online version available through the Gutenberg Project at http://www.gutenberg.org/etext/1497 The specific analogy of the cave comes from Book VII.

65. Please note that I put very strict boundaries around doling out this advice. Going back to Anthony Robbins' Classes of Experience, I will encourage any pursuit as long as it benefits yourself and others, and serves the greater good. I truly believed then and still do now that in this case the father offered a more stable and loving home environment than the mother was capable of providing at that particular time in her life.

66. More women laugh at men's jokes than men laugh at women's. There's an interesting article about hierarchy and laughter in a UK Newspaper. Tracy McVeigh, "It's no joke. We laugh to impress our bosses," *The Observer*, at http://www.guardian.co.uk/uk/2000/oct/08/tracymcveigh.theobserver October 8, 2000.

67. "Domestic Violence: Why do women stay? Why don't they leave?" http://www.womensweb.ca/violence/dv/leave.php extracted October 19, 2009.

68. Robert Gerzon. *Finding Serenity in the Age of Anxiety*. New York: Bantam Books, 1998. p. 279.

69. "Florence Foster Jenkins." *Wikipedia, The Free Encyclopedia*. 9 Nov 2009, 06:13 UTC. 13 Nov 2009 <http://en.wikipedia.org/w/index.php?title=Florence_Foster_Jenkins&oldid=324794652>. A sample of Florence's operatic voice is also available at this site.

70. Tom Kaziol, "Care, Giving and Receiving: Nurturing in the Age of Aging." A Publication of Senior Outreach Ministries ©2004. p. 24. At the time of writing, the Senior's Outreach Manual by Tom Kaziol was available at http://www.katrinadisability.info/PDFsK/care.pdf (November 13, 2009).

71. "success." WordNet® 3.0. Princeton University. 01 Apr. 2009. <Dictionary.com   http://dictionary.reference.com/browse/success>.

72. "failure." Dictionary.com Unabridged (v 1.1). Random House, Inc. 01 Apr. 2009. <Dictionary.com http://dictionary.reference.com/browse/failure >.

73. This concept comes from David Allen. *Getting Things Done: The Art of Stress-Free Productivity*. New York: Penguin Books, 2001. p. 62-81.

74. David Allen defines a "project" as anything that requires more than one action to bring the event to its conclusion.

75. Anthony Robbins. *Unlimited Power*. New York: Fawcett Columbine (Ballantine Books), 1987. p. 11.

76. See *10 Secrets for Success and Inner Peace* by Wayne W. Dyer

77. Ivan R. Misner with Jeff Morris. *Givers Gain: The BNI Story*. Upland, CA: Paradigm Publishing, 2004. p. 78. You can find out more about the organization online at www.bni.com, and you can listen to Dr. Ivan Misner's own podcasts, for free, at http://www.bnipodcast.com.

78. Management Consulting News, "Meeting the MasterMinds: Rosabeth Moss Kanter on Confidence" (date unknown). Extracted January 4, 2010. http://www.managementconsulting-news.com/interviews/kanter_interview.php

PERMISSIONS AND ACKNOWLEDGEMENTS

The poems from Hafiz appearing after the dedication and on pages 2, 90 and 148 are from *The Gift, Poems by Hafiz*, by Daniel Ladinsky. Published by Penguin Compass, copyright © 1999 Daniel Ladinsky and used with his permission.

The excerpt from Dave Lakhani's interview from pages 161-163 is transcribed and presented with permission. The original interview can be found online at http:// exploringthemind.com/ how-to-protect-yourself-from-coercive-groups-and-leaders.

The image of the river on page 214 is called "Un méandre de la Sioule vue de la commune de Queuille, Puy-de-Dôme, région Auvergne" and was taken by Jean-Marc Aubelle. It was released to the public domain by the photographer and is licensed under the Creative Commons Attribution 1.0 Generic license.. The original can be found at http://commons. wikimedia.org/wiki/File:FRANCE_-_Auvergne_-_QUEUILLE_-_Le_ m%C3%A9andre_de_la_Sioule.JPG, extracted November 13, 2009.

The poem "Death Sentence" by Gabrielle Bouliane in Appendix E is transcribed and reprinted here with permission from Gretchen R Bouliane. The original video can be found online at www.youtube.com/ watch?v=gePQuE-7s8c

The three strategies were first introduced to the author through Rosabeth Moss Kanter's book, Confidence: *How Winning and Losing Streaks Begin and End*. The book that you now hold in your hands, *The Three Strategies of the Unstoppable Woman*, extracts Kanter's three cornerstones of confidence and overlays them directly over the female journey to success. The author is indebted to Rosabeth Moss Kanter for the clear articulation of these three cornerstones.

The author would also like to thank the following for their support:

- The Pineview gang

- The Facebook friends and fans

- The Twits (errrr Twitters) who followed with genuine interest

- The past and present mastermind group members

- And of course all the clan members of the family (Santowski's, Anderson's and Cummings').

Specifically, she would like to thank Vincent Cummings, her husband, who really made mountains move so that she could write this book.

5596952R0

Made in the USA
Charleston, SC
08 July 2010